Fabric Lovers
HOLIDAY CREATIONS

Oxmoor
House.

Fabric Lovers Holiday Creations
from the *Fun with Fabric* series
©1999 by Oxmoor House, Inc.
Book Division of Southern Progress Corporation
P.O. Box 2463, Birmingham, Alabama 35201

Published by Oxmoor House, Inc., and
Leisure Arts, Inc.

Library of Congress Catalog Card Number: 99-74813
Hardcover ISBN: 0-8487-1908-5
Softcover ISBN: 0-8487-1909-3
Printed in the United States of America
First Printing 1999

Editor-in-Chief: Nancy Fitzpatrick Wyatt
Senior Crafts Editor: Susan Ramey Cleveland
Senior Editor, Copy and Homes: Olivia Kindig Wells
Art Director: James Boone

Fabric Lovers Holiday Creations

Editor: Catherine Corbett Fowler
Copy Editor: L. Amanda Owens
Senior Photographer: John O'Hagan
Photo Stylist: Linda Baltzell Wright
Illustrator: Kelly Davis
Contributing Designer: Carol Damsky
Publishing Systems Administrator: Rick Tucker
Production and Distribution Director: Phillip Lee
Associate Production Manager: Theresa L. Beste
Production Assistant: Faye Porter Bonner

We're Here for You!
We at Oxmoor House are dedicated to serving you
with reliable information that expands your imagi-
nation and enriches your life. We welcome your
comments and suggestions. Please write us at:

Oxmoor House, Inc.
Editor, *Fabric Lovers Holiday Creations*
2100 Lakeshore Drive
Birmingham, AL 35209

To order additional publications, call
1-205-877-6560.

*C*ontents

Holiday Table

Holidays at Home

Acknowledgments

Page 31

Page 70

Page 116

3

Introduction

*I*t can be such fun to craft handmade items that help make seasonal celebrations real occasions. But holidays are also busy events. With all the other preparations involved, there simply isn't much time or energy left for thinking of clever gifts and decorations. *Fabric Lovers Holiday Creations* takes care of all that for you. You'll discover page after page of imaginative ideas for festivities—from January through December. So browse through the book, find the holiday that's just around the corner, and begin planning the wonderful items you want to create.

The mere mention of an upcoming holiday will likely set you to wondering about presents for family and friends. In **Gifts for Holidays**, you will find pages overflowing with wonderfully easy-to-make items to thrill all your loved ones.

Because so many festivities are planned around dining, **Holiday Table** is devoted entirely to projects that will make the setting as memorable as the meal.

Surround your family with decorations that will become a treasured part of holiday celebrations. **Holidays at Home** contains more than 20 memory-making projects.

5

General *Instructions*

In this handy guide, you'll find lots of tips and techniques to help you create picture-perfect projects.

Wearables and Linens

• Wash, dry, and press all fabric items before beginning a project. Do not use fabric softener in the washer or the dryer. Prewashing removes sizing and allows fusible web, fabric paint, and fabric glue to adhere better.

• Because garments and linens receive so much wear and tear, you may want to use a heavyweight web (unless the fabric is very lightweight) when constructing or embellishing one of these items.

• Special care should be used when laundering handmade items. It's best to hand-wash them and then hang them to dry or spot-clean them with soap and water.

Making a Multilooped Bow

For an 8"-wide bow, you will need 4 yards of wire-edged ribbon. To make the bow, measure 4" from one end of the ribbon. Pinch the ribbon between your forefinger and thumb (this will be the center point of the bow). Make a 4" loop and pinch the ribbon again at the center (Diagram 1). Twist the ribbon one-half turn and make a loop on the opposite side. Continue in this manner to make 5 loops on each side (Diagram 2). Fold a 9" length of florist's wire over the center of the bow. Fold

the bow in half across the wire. Holding the bow securely, twist the wire ends together (Diagram 3). Fluff the bow by pulling firmly on the loops.

Fusing Basics

1. Place the web side of the fusible web on the wrong side of the fabric. Press for 5 seconds with a hot, dry iron. Let the fabric cool. (If some fusible web sticks to your iron, remove it with a hot iron cleaner, which is available in most notion departments of fabric and crafts stores.)

2. Remove the paper backing. Position the fused fabric, web side down, on the project. (Fusible items can be held temporarily in place by "touch basting." Touch the item to be fused with the tip of the iron only. If the item is not in the desired position, it can be lifted and repositioned.)

3. To fuse, cover the fabric with a damp pressing cloth. Using an iron heated to the wool setting, press firmly for 10 seconds. (Heavier fabrics require more time.) Repeat, lifting and overlapping the iron until all the fabric is fused.

4. Remove the pressing cloth and iron the fabric to eliminate excess moisture.

Using Dimensional Paint

• Practice painting on scrap fabric.

• To keep the paint flowing smoothly, turn the bottle upside down and let the paint fill the tip before each use.

• Clean the bottle tip often with paper towels.

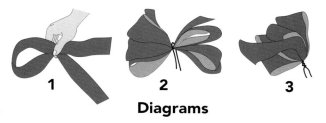

1   **2**   **3**

Diagrams

- If the bottle tip becomes clogged, insert a straight pin into the tip opening.
- When painting lines or painting over appliqués, keep the bottle tip in contact with the fabric, applying a thick line of paint over the drawn line or the raw edge of the appliqué.
- To correct a mistake, use a paring knife to gently scrape the excess paint from the fabric before it dries. Carefully remove the stain with nonacetone nail polish remover. An error may also be camouflaged by incorporating it into the project design.
- Before adding trims, lay the garment flat for at least 24 hours to ensure that the paint is sufficiently set.

Embroidery Stitches

Straightstitch

Knot one end of the floss. Push the needle up from the wrong side of the fabric. Insert the needle up and down in the fabric as shown at right. The stitch lengths may be varied as desired.

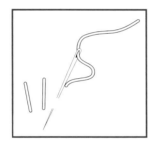

Running Stitch

Knot one end of the floss. Bring the needle up from the wrong side of the fabric. Insert the needle back down into the fabric and then come up from the wrong side, one stitch space away. Continue stitching in this manner.

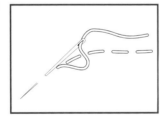

Blanket Stitch

Knot one end of the floss. Push the needle up from the wrong side of the fabric, even with the edge of the appliqué. Insert the needle into the appliqué and then come up at the edge again, keeping the floss below the point of the needle. Continue stitching in this manner, keeping the stitches even.

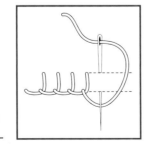

Backstitch

Knot one end of the floss. Push the needle up from the wrong side of the fabric. Take a stitch back approximately ⅛", bringing the needle out again ⅛" forward. Continue inserting the needle in the end of the last stitch and bringing it out one stitch ahead. The stitches on the underside will be twice as long as those on the top.

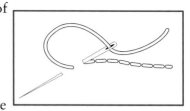

French Knot

Knot one end of the floss. Push the needle up from the wrong side of the fabric. Wrap the end of the floss closest to the fabric around the needle twice (A). Reinsert the needle into the fabric next to the first stitch, holding the end of the floss with your free hand (B). Tighten the knot; then pull the needle through, holding the floss until it must be released (C).

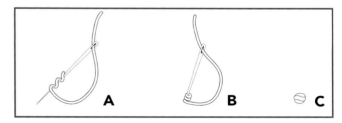

Perfect Patterns

- If a pattern has an asymmetrical or one-way design, a finished appliqué will be a mirror image of the pattern. So if a pattern points left, the appliqué will point right. **In this book, patterns are reversed as necessary.**
- When an entire pattern is shown, simply place tracing paper over the pattern and trace the pattern. Cut out the pattern. For a more durable pattern, use a permanent pen to trace the pattern onto template plastic; then cut out the pattern.
- When only half of a pattern is shown, fold the tracing paper in half; place the fold in the paper along the fold line of the pattern. Trace the pattern half; turn the folded paper over and draw over the traced lines on the remaining side of the paper. Unfold the paper and cut out the pattern.

Embellishment
Techniques

The purpose of an embellishment is to add polish to your project. And, sometimes, the embellishment actually helps secure elements of the design so that the project will hold up to repeated use.

Washable fabric paint makes a good no-sew finish. Available at crafts stores, these paints come in squeeze tubes that allow you to outline an appliqué with a thin line of paint. Place cardboard under the appliqué to prevent seepage and follow the manufacturer's directions for drying time (some paints require several days to set.) Most manufacturers recommend washing the finished project in warm water.

Rickrack is available in a variety of sizes, from very thin to very fat. It can be used as a decorative element, as in Hanukkah Pillow on page 40, or as a finish to a raw edge, as shown here.

Buttons, trims, and tassels, such as those shown here, are usually purely decorative, but they certainly give projects a great deal of finesse.

Embroidery stitches serve three functions: They can be used as details, such as these eyes and legs; can add a whimsical decorative element to a project; and can help secure appliqués and trims.

Closely stitched zigzags—or **satin stitching**—give shapes stong definition and completely encase raw edges, which secures appliqués.

Cording defines both form and function. It has been used at least three different ways in this book: for lettering, as shown above; for tying a package (see Wonderful Wine Bags on page 50); and for edging a pillow (see Pillow for Pop on page 24).

Page 31

Page 40

Page 48

Page 14

Gifts for Holidays

*W*ant to send an extra-special Valentine to your mom? Valentine Photo Mats (page 12) will put a smile on her face. Stumped for a gift for Dad for Father's Day? Pillow for Pop (page 24) has a nifty pocket for keeping his television remote right at hand. Need a quick hostess gift? Sweet-smelling Christmas Coasters (page 36) stitch up in no time.

Valentine Photo Mats

Send a Valentine that is sure to stand out from the rest. One of these lightweight thin frames is just right for mailing in a regular envelope.

Materials

For each:
Craft knife
Cutting mat
Ruler
8" x 10" piece mat board
Paintbrush
Craft glue
2 (18") lengths ¾"-wide grosgrain ribbon
8" x 10" piece felt
4" x 6" photo
Cellophane tape

For blue frame:
10" x 12" piece blue print fabric
1¼ yards wide rickrack
4 (⅞") heart buttons

For red heart or red gingham frame:
10" x 12" piece red print fabric
Buttons: 4 (⅞") heart buttons, approximately 64 (⅜" to ⅝")

Instructions

1. **For each,** using craft knife, cutting mat, and ruler, cut 3" x 5" opening in center of mat board.

2. Using paintbrush, apply thin coat of craft glue to 1 side of mat board. Center mat board, glue side down, on wrong side of fabric. Smooth out wrinkles with fingers. With tip of sharp scissors, poke hole in center of fabric in frame opening. From poked hole, cut slits in fabric to within ⅛" of each corner of opening. Glue excess fabric along opening edges and outer edges to back of frame, trimming if necessary. Let dry.

3. Referring to photo, glue 1 end of each ribbon length to top edge on back of frame, positioning ribbons at angle. Let dry.

4. For blue frame, cut 2 (12") lengths and 2 (10") lengths from rickrack. Glue 1 (12") length along top edge of frame, positioning rickrack approximately ¾" from edge of frame and wrapping ends to back. Glue in place. Repeat to glue remaining 12" length to bottom edge of frame. Glue 1 (10") length along 1 side of frame, positioning rickrack approximately ⅜" from edge of frame and wrapping ends to back. Glue in place. Let dry.

5. For each, cut 3" x 5" opening in center of felt piece. Apply 1 coat of fabric glue to back of frame.

Center felt on back of frame and press into glue. Let dry.

6. Referring to photo, glue 1 heart button in each corner of frame opening. Let dry. Tie free ends of ribbon in bow, approximately 2½" above top edge of frame.

7. For red heart and red gingham frames, glue remaining buttons around edges of frame. Let dry.

8. For each, center photo in opening and tape to back of frame.

Easy Easter Totes

Why put all your eggs in one container when you can choose to carry your treats in a bucket, a bag, or a basket.

Bunny Bucket and Spring Sacks

Materials

For each:
Paper-backed fusible web scraps
Fabric scraps
For bucket:
White felt scrap
White metal bucket
Tacky glue
2 (½") buttons
For 1 sack:
Paper gift bag with handles: green or white

Instructions for bucket

Press fusible web scraps onto wrong sides of fabric scraps and onto 1 side of felt scrap. Trace 2 large bunny shapes (see page 16) onto paper side of fabric scraps. Draw 2 (¾"-diameter) circles on paper side of felt scrap. Cut out shapes along pattern lines. Remove paper backing. Referring to photo, fuse bunny shapes to bucket. Fuse 1 felt circle tail in place on each bunny. Glue 1 button eye in place on each bunny.

Instructions for sack

Press fusible web scraps to wrong sides of fabric scraps. Transfer desired patterns (see page 16) to paper side of fabric scraps. Cut out shapes along pattern lines. Remove paper backing. Referring to photo, fuse fabric shapes to bag.

Fabric Basket
(shown on page 17)

Materials

Pinking shears
Easter print fabric: 22"-diameter circle,
 3¼" x 12½" strip
Empty, clean 26-ounce coffee can
Rubber band
1¼ yards each grosgrain ribbons: ⅜"-wide purple,
 ⅝"-wide pink
Craft glue
1¼" x 12" strip cardboard
Hot-glue gun and glue sticks

Instructions

1. Using pinking shears, trim edges of fabric circle. Place fabric circle facedown and center coffee can on circle. Pull fabric up around coffee can and place rubber band around top of can to hold fabric in place. Adjust gathers as desired.
2. Stack purple ribbon on top of pink ribbon. Holding ribbons together as one, tie in bow around top of can, covering rubber band.
3. To make handle, apply thin coat of craft glue to 1 side of cardboard strip. Center cardboard

strip, glue side down, on wrong side of fabric strip. Smooth any wrinkles, using fingers. Apply thin coat of craft glue to back of cardboard strip. Fold long edges of fabric to back of cardboard strip, overlapping edges slightly. Apply craft glue to overlap to secure. Let dry. Bend handle slightly. Hot-glue ends of handle to opposite inside top edges of coffee can.

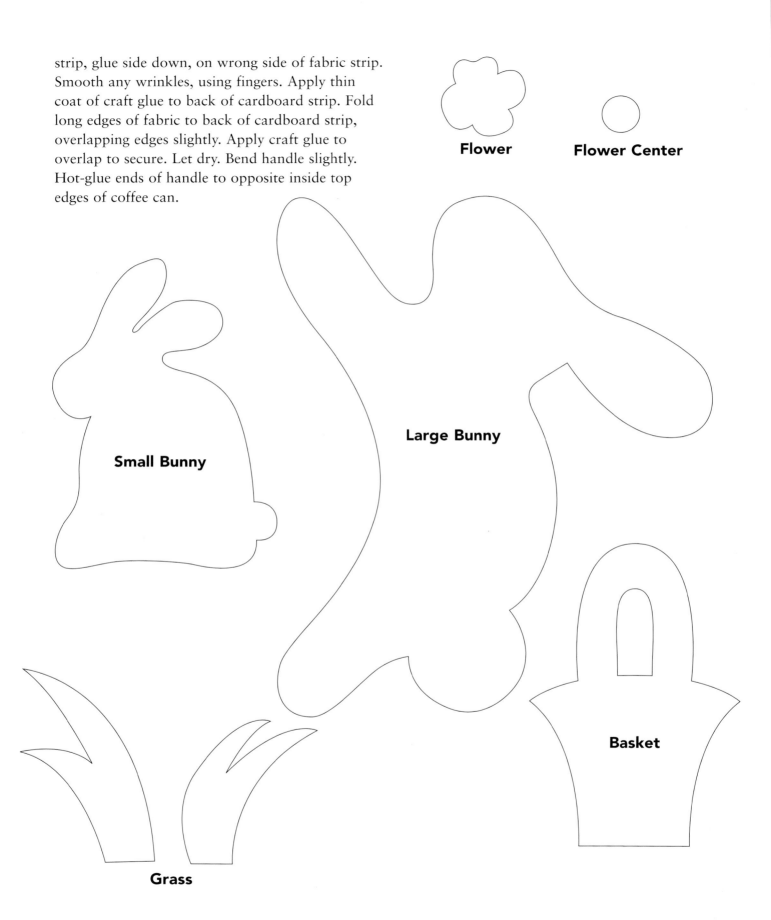

Flower

Flower Center

Small Bunny

Large Bunny

Basket

Grass

*E*aster
Baby Outfit

Don't spend a fortune on an Easter playsuit that your baby will get to wear only once. For pennies you can create this darling egg-embellished Onesie.

Materials

Purchased Onesie or baby T-shirt
Pastel cotton fabric scraps
Paper-backed fusible web scraps
Cardboard covered with waxed paper
Fabric paints in bottles with tips: white pearl, green

Instructions

1. Wash and dry Onesie and fabrics; do not use fabric softener in washer or dryer. Press Onesie and fabrics to remove any wrinkles.

2. Press fusible web scraps onto wrong side of fabric scraps. Transfer egg pattern to paper side of fabric scraps and cut 3. Cut out shapes along pattern lines. Remove paper backing.

3. Referring to photo for placement, fuse eggs to front of Onesie. Insert cardboard covered with waxed paper inside Onesie. Referring to photo, use white pearl fabric paint to decorate each egg. Let dry. Use green paint to make grass. Let dry.

4. Do not wash Onesie for 24 hours. To launder, wash by hand and hang to dry.

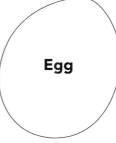

Egg

Dressy Bunnies

These bunny dolls will be the best surprise in your little girl's Easter basket. Make the no-sew outfits in her favorite colors.

Materials

For each:
Low-temp glue gun and glue sticks
1" white pom-pom
Powdered blusher
Pinking shears
Pink fabric scraps

For small bunny:
Purchased muslin bunny (11" from tip of ear to
    bottom of foot)
Cotton print fabric: 1 (5" x 11") rectangle,
    1 (2½" x 6") strip
Satin ribbons: 1 (16") length ⅜"-wide, 2 (6")
    lengths ⅛"-wide
Ribbon rose

For large bunny:
Purchased muslin bunny (17" from tip of ear to
    bottom of foot)
Cotton print fabric: 1 (7" x 18") rectangle,
    1 (2½" x 15") strip
9 (6") lengths ⅛"-wide satin ribbon in variety of
    colors

Instructions

1. **For each,** fold 1 long edge of fabric rectangle under ¼" and press. Open fold, apply glue, and refold. Overlap short ends of fabric rectangle to form tube; glue edges. Slip bunny inside fabric tube. Align raw edge of fabric tube under bunny arms, positioning seam at center back. Working in sections, gather raw edge of fabric and glue to bunny under arms. Glue center back and center front of folded open end of fabric tube to bunny between legs, overlapping slightly. Use small dot of glue to glue outer edge of each resulting leg opening to bunny leg. (Most of leg openings will remain free.)

2. Place bunny in sitting position. Glue pom-pom to back center seam for tail. Use powdered blusher for cheeks. Using pinking shears and referring to photo, cut 2 inner ear shapes from pink fabric scraps. Center and glue inner ears in place on bunny ears.

3. Fold fabric strip in half lengthwise and press. Open fold. Fold each long raw edge to center and press. Refold strip along center fold, enclosing raw edges. Insert tip of glue gun between layers and lightly glue layers together.

4. **For small bunny,** cut folded strip in half. Glue 1 strip in place over each shoulder for straps. Cover ends of shoulder straps and gathered edge of outfit with ⅜" satin ribbon, overlapping ends and trimming excess. Glue in place. Tie remaining ⅜" ribbon in bow and trim ends, if necessary. Glue bow to front of bunny. Holding ⅛" ribbon lengths together as one, tie knot in center and trim ends, if necessary. Glue center knot and ribbon rose to top of bunny head in front of 1 ear (see photo).

5. **For large bunny,** from folded strip, cut 2 (4") lengths and 1 (7") length. Glue 1 (4") piece over each shoulder for straps. Cover ends of shoulder straps and gathered edge of outfit with 7" length. Glue in place, overlapping ends at back. Tie knot at ends of each satin ribbon length. Holding all lengths as one, tie knot in center. Glue center knot to top of bunny head between ears (see photo).

Mother's Day
Garden Tote

Whether Mom is a serious gardener or just a weekend hobbyist, she's bound to appreciate this botanical bag. She'll find it handy for storing her tools between plantings, or she may prefer to use it as an oversize purse.

Materials

¾ yard floral print fabric*
Canvas tote with pockets*
¾ yard 17"-wide paper-backed fusible web
Thread to match fabric
5 or 6 ladybug buttons
Fabric glue
Note: Look for print fabric with motifs that are slightly smaller than pockets. For canvas tote bag, write to BagWorks at 3301-C South Cravens Road, Fort Worth, Texas 76119 or call (817) 446-8105.

Instructions

Wash and dry floral fabric; do not use fabric softener in washer or dryer. Press fabric to remove any wrinkles. Referring to photo, cut rectangles from fabric, each small enough to fit on top of pockets. (Pockets on our tote are 6" x 8"; fabric rectangles are 5" x 7".) Using 1 fabric rectangle as guide, cut rectangles from fusible web. Press 1 fusible web rectangle to wrong side of each fabric rectangle. Referring to photo, position fabric rectangles on tote pockets and fuse in place. Positioning arm of sewing machine between pocket and body of tote, stitch along edges of each fabric rectangle. Referring to photo, arrange and glue ladybug buttons on tote.

Package It

For a generous presentation, fill the tote with an assortment of garden gifts. Tuck small plants or flowers, such as pansies or ivy, into the pockets. Then fill the inside of the tote with a large plant, such as a fern. Or stuff the pockets with small tools and the inside of the tote with tissue-wrapped terra-cotta pots. Finish by tying a bow and a gift card to the handles of the tote.

Pillow
for Pop

The king of the remote need no longer search for his electronic scepter; it will be right at hand inside this handsome pillow.

Materials

½ yard 54"-wide fabric
Iron-on transfer (See Step 2.)
2 yards cording with lip
Straight pins
Thread to match fabric
Sewing machine with zipper foot
¾"-wide paper-backed fusible web tape
Hand-sewing needle
16" square pillow form

Instructions

1. From fabric, cut 3 (18") squares.

2. Have local copy shop create iron-on transfer of pattern (see page 26). Center and press iron-on transfer on right side of 1 fabric piece. (Many copy shops will also press transfers onto fabric for you. You may prefer for them to do this step in order to assure that all of image transfers properly.)

3. Pin cording to right side of pillow cover front, aligning lip with raw edge of fabric. (At corners, clip cording lip to ease.) Using zipper foot, stitch as close to cording as possible.

4. For pocket, turn under 6" along 1 edge of 1 remaining fabric piece; press. Use paper-backed fusible web tape to fuse folded edge in place. With right sides up and raw edges aligned, stack pocket piece on remaining fabric piece. Baste pocket in place along raw edges.

5. With right sides facing and raw edges aligned, stitch pillow cover front and back together, sandwiching cording and pocket between layers and leaving opening for inserting pillow form. Clip corners. Press seams. Turn pillow cover right side out and press.

6. Insert pillow form into cover. Using needle and thread, slipstitch opening closed.

Dad's couch pouch

Independence Day
Apron

*Three cheers for good old American ingenuity!
This clever apron is made by piecing together lengths of
red, white, and blue ribbons.*

Materials

Liquid ravel preventer

Grosgrain ribbons: ⅜"-wide red with stars*;
3 (3½") lengths 1"-wide blue with dots; 2 (5")
lengths ⅜"-wide silver metallic; 2 (3") lengths
1"-wide red-and-white stripe; 4 (1") lengths
⅜"-wide blue with dots, cut with dots centered;
3 (3½") lengths ⅜"-wide blue solid; 1 (2")
length ⅝"-wide blue solid

Thread: monofilament, white

Purchased white bib apron

Fabric glue

*Note: To determine exact yardage needed,
measure across top of bib and along side edges and
neck strap.

Instructions

Note: Coat cut ends of all ribbon pieces with liquid ravel preventer. Use monofilament thread in top of sewing machine and white thread in bobbin for all stitching.

1. Cut length of ⅜"-wide red star ribbon to fit across top of bib. With edges aligned, topstitch ribbon length in place on bib. Turn under ¼" at 1 end of remaining ⅜"-wide red star ribbon. With edges aligned and beginning at waist, topstitch ribbon along 1 side of apron, around neck strap, and down opposite side of apron, stopping 1" from waist. Trim ribbon 1¼" from end of stitching; turn cut end of ribbon under ¼" and then continue stitching ribbon in place.

2. For spatula, with 1"-wide blue dotted ribbon pieces side by side, overlap long edges slightly and zigzag together. Referring to photo on page 27, position spatula pieces on bib as follows: 3½" length of overlapped blue dotted ribbon, 1 (5") length of silver ribbon (slip top raw edge of silver ribbon under blue ribon), 1 (3") length red-and-white stripe ribbon, and 2 (1") lengths of ⅜"-wide blue dotted ribbon. Glue ribbon pieces to bib.

3. For fork tines, cut 1 end of each piece of ⅜"-wide solid blue ribbon in point. Referring to photo, position fork pieces on bib as above, substituting tines and 2" length of ⅝"-wide solid blue ribbon for spatula ribbon piece. Glue pieces to bib.

4. Topstitch utensils in place.

Happy Spider
Halloween Shirt

You'll love being trapped in this spiderweb! A scrap of fabric, a little fabric paint, and 30 minutes of your time are all it takes to make this playful Halloween shirt.

Materials

Purchased orange T-shirt
Purple fabric scrap
Disappearing-ink fabric marker
Paper-backed fusible web scrap
Dimensional fabric paints: white, red, black
2 (12-mm) wiggle eyes
E-6000 glue

Instructions

1. Wash, dry, and press T-shirt and fabric scrap; do not use fabric softener in washer or dryer. Using disappearing-ink marker, transfer spiderweb (see page 30) onto center front of T-shirt.

2. Press paper-backed fusible web scrap to wrong side of purple fabric scrap. Transfer 1 spider body pattern and 8 foot patterns (see page 30) to paper side of fabric. Cut out shapes along pattern lines. Remove paper backing. Referring to photo, fuse spider body to center of spiderweb; fuse feet in place, approximately 2" from body.

3. Using white paint, trace marked spiderweb. Let dry. Using red paint, draw smiling spider mouth. Let dry. Using black paint, add spider legs. Let dry. Glue wiggle eyes in place on spider. Let dry.

4. Do not wash T-shirt for 24 hours. To launder, wash by hand and hang to dry.

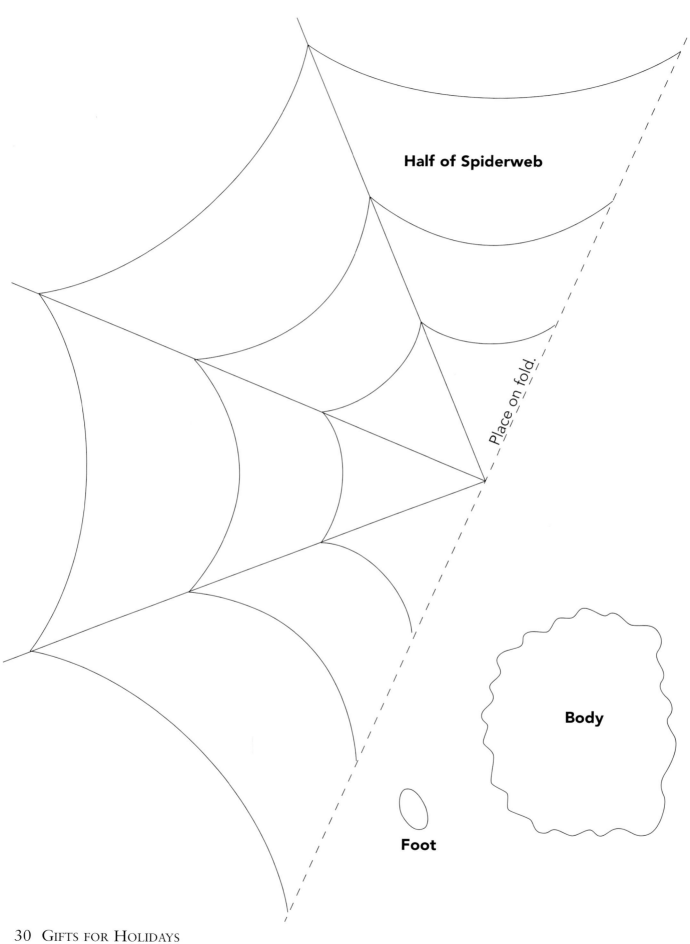

Half of Spiderweb

Place on fold.

Body

Foot

Jack-o'-lantern
Tote Bags

Whether you plan to do a little trick-or-treating or a lot, the friendly faces on these goodie bags will guarantee successful gathering.

Materials

For each:
Pinking shears
Thread: orange, green
Heavy-duty paper-backed fusible web

For large tote:
Duck cloth: 15" x 40" piece orange, black scraps
4 (24") lengths 1"-wide green grosgrain ribbon

For small tote:
Duck cloth: 7½" x 20" piece orange, black scraps
2 (12") lengths ⅝"-wide green grosgrain ribbon

Instructions

1. **For each,** trim short ends of orange fabric piece with pinking shears. Fold fabric in half, with short ends together. Stitch fabric along long sides, using ½" seam allowance. Turn right side out and press.

2. **For large bag,** fold top raw edge under 2"; press. Cut 2 (1" x 24") lengths from fusible web. Press 1 fusible web length each onto 1 side of 2 ribbon lengths. Remove paper backing. Fuse 1 web-covered ribbon length to each plain ribbon length. Zigzag along long edges of both ribbon lengths to secure. Pin ends of 1 ribbon length to inside top of bag front, positioning ribbon ends approximately 4" from outer edges. Repeat with remaining ribbon length on inside top of bag back.

3. **For small bag,** fold top raw edge under 1½"; press. Pin 1 ribbon length to inside top of bag front, positioning ribbon ends approximately 1½" from outer edges. Repeat with remaining ribbon length on inside top of bag back.

4. **For each,** stitch along top and bottom edges of folded hem, catching ribbon handles in stitching.

5. Press paper-backed fusible web onto wrong side of black fabric scraps. Transfer corresponding patterns for each bag to paper side of fabric. Cut 1 mouth and 3 triangles along pattern lines. Remove paper backing.

6. Referring to photo on page 31 for positioning, fuse mouth and triangle eyes and nose in place.

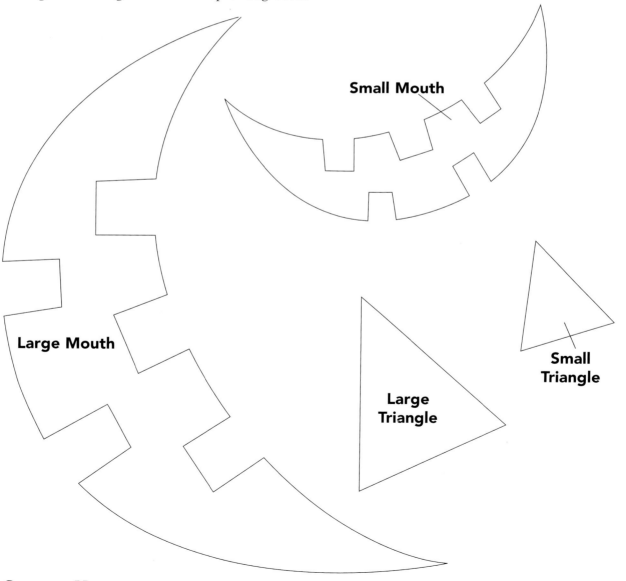

Small Mouth

Large Mouth

Large Triangle

Small Triangle

Peppermint
Stress-Relief Collar

After a frantic day of Christmas shopping for others, spend a relaxing evening pampering yourself. Heat this velvet collar in the microwave. Then place it around your neck, lie back, close your eyes, and deeply breathe in the soothing scent of peppermint.

Materials

½ yard velvet
Disappearing-ink fabric marker
Straight pins
1¼ yards lace
Thread to match velvet
1 pound uncooked pearl tapioca*
Peppermint essential oil
Funnel
Hand-sewing needle
*Note: Pearl tapioca is available in grocery and health food stores. "Minute" tapioca is not suitable for this project.

Instructions

Note: Seam allowances are ¼".

1. Transfer collar pattern to velvet and cut 2. Using disappearing-ink marker, transfer topstitching lines from pattern to 1 collar piece.

2. Beginning and ending ¼" from center front edges of collar, pin lace to right side of 1 collar piece along center front and outer edges only, aligning bound edge of lace with raw edge of collar. Adjust lace so that motifs match at front. Baste lace to collar along seam line.

3. With right sides facing and raw edges aligned, stitch collar pieces together, leaving 3" opening at center back. Clip curves. Turn collar and press lightly, using scrap piece of velvet on ironing board to prevent crushing velvet collar. Topstitch along transferred lines.

4. Sprinkle tapioca with few drops of peppermint oil. (Essential oil is highly concentrated, so only small amount is needed.) Using funnel and working over bowl, fill collar and evenly distributing tapioca into channels. Slipstitch collar opening closed.

5. To use, heat collar on high in microwave for approximately 1 minute. Do not overheat. Collar will stay warm for 15 to 20 minutes.

Essential Oil Guide

For our stress-relief collar, we suggested scenting it with peppermint essential oil. Not only is this a wonderful holiday fragrance, but also it is said to reduce fatigue. However, you may prefer to try other aromas. Use this handy guide for selecting the essential oils with the aromatherapy benefits you desire.

Essential Oil	Benefits
Lemongrass	Refreshes and clears the mind.
Orange	Refreshes and clears the mind.
Tangerine	Instills feelings of pleasure and happiness.
Lavender	Instills feeling of happiness; helps you sleep.
Sandalwood	Promotes romance and passion.
Clove	Promotes relaxation and romance.
Cinnamon	Promotes romance.
Vanilla	Promotes romance.
Jasmine	Improves overall mood.
Cedarwood	Instills tranquility and inner peace.
Chamomile	Instills tranquility and inner peace.

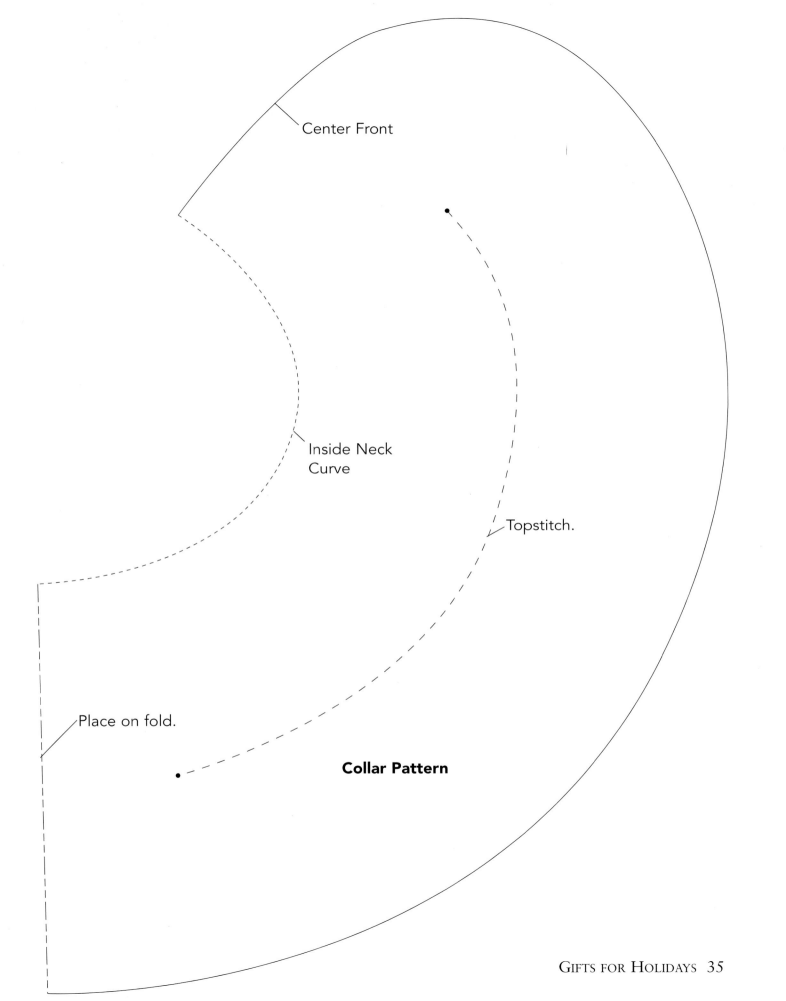

Center Front

Inside Neck
Curve

Topstitch.

Place on fold.

Collar Pattern

Christmas Coasters

Need a quick gift? These merry little coasters stitch up in no time, making them an ideal last-minute hostess gift.

Materials

(for 6 coasters)

⅓ yard Christmas fabric (If necessary, allow extra yardage for centering design motifs.)

Polyester batting

Thread to match fabric

6 tablespoons whole cloves

3 cinnamon sticks, broken into small pieces

Hand-sewing needle

Ribbon (optional)

Instructions

From fabric, cut 12 (5") squares. From batting, cut 6 (5") squares. **For each,** layer 2 fabric squares (with right sides together) and top with batting square. Using ¼" seam allowance, stitch along sides, leaving 2" opening for turning. Trim batting close to stitching. Trim corners, turn, and press. Combine cloves and cinnamon stick pieces. Spoon approximately 1 tablespoon of spice mixture into coaster. Slipstitch opening closed. Tie stack of coasters together with ribbon, if desired.

Herbal Bathtub Tea

There's more than one way to enjoy a spot of tea. Dip one of these herbal tea bags in a tub of warm water and indulge yourself in a lavender-scented bath.

Materials

(for 1 tea bag)
Pinking shears
Muslin scraps
White thread
Dried lavender
7" length narrow gold cording
Red or green decorative tassel*
Fabric glue
*Note: We used tassels cut from a row of fringed trim.

Instructions

Using pinking shears, cut 2 (4") squares from muslin scraps. Aligning edges, stack and topstitch squares together along 3 sides, using 5/8" seam allowance. Fill bag with dried lavender. Center 1 end of cording in top of bag between layers of muslin. Topstitch, using 5/8" seam allowance and catching cording in seam. Tie knot in free end of cording. Glue decorative tassel at center top of tea bag. To use, steep tea bag in hot bath to release lavender scent.

Tree-Trimmed *Sweatshirt*

The simplicity of this shirt, both in design and construction, will make it a favorite addition to your holiday wardrobe.

Materials
Paper-backed fusible web
3 different plaid flannel scraps
Purchased sweatshirt
Thread to match fabrics
Hand-sewing needle
3 (½") decorative buttons

Instructions
Press paper-backed fusible web onto wrong side of flannel scraps. Trace tree pattern onto paper side of each flannel scrap. Cut out shapes along pattern lines. Remove paper backing. Arrange trees on sweatshirt front as desired. Fuse in place. Using medium-width zigzag, stitch along edges of trees. Sew 1 button to top of each tree.

Tree

Hanukkah
Pillow

A shining Star of David on a soft blue velvet background makes an elegant pillow that reflects the beauty of the Jewish festival.

Materials

Tracing paper
½ yard blue velvet
Straight pins
Dressmaker's pen
2 (29¼") lengths large silver rickrack
Thread: silver metallic, white, blue
Large embroidery needle
4 silver tassels
16" square pillow form
Hand-sewing needle

Instructions

1. From tracing paper, cut 2 (9") equilateral triangles. From velvet, cut 2 (17") squares.
2. Center triangle patterns in shape of Star of David on right side of 1 velvet square. Pin in place. Using dressmaker's pen, lightly trace each triangle pattern. Remove patterns. Fold each rickrack length into 9" equilateral triangle shape.

Position rickrack triangles on traced star shape, interweaving rickrack over and under where pieces overlap. Pin rickrack in place. Using silver thread in top of sewing machine and white thread in bobbin, stitch rickrack to velvet square.
3. With right sides facing and edges aligned, pin velvet squares together. Using blue thread, stitch pillow cover front and back together, using ½" seam allowance and leaving ¼" opening at each corner and 5" opening along bottom for inserting pillow form.
4. Turn velvet pillow cover right side out. Thread large embroidery needle with loop of 1 tassel. Use needle to insert tassel into 1 corner of pillow cover. Pull loop through to inside of pillow cover and knot securely in place. Repeat to attach 1 tassel to each corner.
5. Insert pillow form into cover. Slipstitch opening closed.

Poinsettia Pot Wraps

A clever embellishment often turns a good gift into a great gift. These charming burlap and jingle bell pot wraps are a wonderful finishing touch for holiday plants.

Materials

(for 1 wrapper)

Holiday plant in plastic pot*
Tape measure
Scrap paper
Cellophane tape
String
Pencil
Pushpin
1 yard burlap: red, green, or cream
Hot-glue gun and glue sticks
13- and 20-mm silver jingle bells
*Note: If pot has foil wrapper, trim it even with top edge of pot. Otherwise, wrap pot in plastic wrap or aluminum foil and secure with masking tape.

Instructions

1. To determine diameter for wrapper, measure from inside of pot at soil line, up over rim of pot, down side, under bottom of pot, and around to opposite side soil line. Tape sheets of paper together to make square equal to determined diameter. Fold paper square in half and then in fourths.

2. To make pattern, divide diameter in half to find radius. Tie 1 end of string to pencil. Insert pushpin into string at distance from pencil equal to determined radius; then insert pushpin at folded corner

of paper. Pull string taut and draw arc from edge to edge. Cut out pattern. Unfold. Center pattern on burlap and cut out.

3. Center pot on burlap. Pull burlap up, fold excess over rim, pleating as necessary to ease fullness. Glue excess to inside edge of pot just above soil line. Glue jingle bells to sides of burlap-covered pot as desired.

Festive Frames

Cover purchased picture frames with seasonal fabrics to create your own holiday photo gallery.

Materials (for 1 frame)

Purchased picture frame with wide, smooth border
Sponge paintbrush
Craft glue
Fabric (Yardage equals size of frame plus 1½" on each side.)
Putty knife

Instructions

Remove backing, fillers, and glass from frame. Using sponge brush, apply thin layer of craft glue to front surface of frame only. Center frame face-down on wrong side of fabric. Turn frame over and smooth fabric with putty knife. With tip of sharp scissors, poke hole in center of fabric in frame opening. From poked hole, cut slits in fabric to within ⅛" of each corner of opening. Glue excess fabric along opening edges and outer edges to back of frame, trimming if necessary. For crisp edges, use putty knife to press fabric to frame. Let dry. Reassemble frame, including desired photo.

Christmas Carryall

The holiday season is one party after another, and you never go empty-handed. This colorful ornament tote bag is a festive way to transport all of your holiday gifts and goodies.

Materials

6 or 7 different red and green cotton fabric scraps
Ruler
Fabric marking pencil
⅝"-wide paper-backed fusible web tape
Clipboard
Pressing paper or aluminum foil
3 (6") squares paper-backed fusible web
Canvas tote bag*
Straight pins
1¾ yards ⅝"-wide red grosgrain ribbon
Fabric glue
3 gold buttons in desired size
*Note: For canvas tote bag, write to BagWorks at 3301-C South Cravens Road, Fort Worth, Texas 76119 or call (817) 446-8105.

Instructions

1. Cut 3 (6") squares from fabric scraps. Using ruler and fabric marking pencil, measure and mark vertical lines at ½" intervals on back of fabric squares. Starting at 1 side, cut along marked lines, stopping ½" from opposite edge.

2. Press 18 (6") lengths of fusible web tape to back of remaining fabric scraps. Using edges of web tape as guide, cut strips from fabric scraps. Remove paper backing.

3. Attach uncut edge of 1 fabric square to clipboard. Working from top to bottom, weave 6 fabric strips over and under cut sections of fabric square (see photo). Remove from clipboard. Place woven square onto pressing paper or aluminum foil and press to fuse fabric strips in place. Repeat with remaining squares.

4. Press 1 fusible web square onto wrong side of each woven square. Draw 1 (5"-diameter) circle on paper side of each woven square. Cut out circles along marked lines. Referring to photo for placement, position ornaments on 1 side of bag. Pin ornaments in place.

5. From red ribbon, cut 2 (10") lengths and 1 (6") length. From web tape, cut 2 (8") lengths and 1 (4") length. With 1 cut end aligned, press 1 (8") web tape length onto each 10" ribbon length and 1 (4") web tape length onto each 6" ribbon length. Remove paper backing.

6. Referring to photo, tuck webbing end of 1 ribbon under each ornament at center top. Fuse ornaments and ribbons in place. Trim free end of each ribbon in V; fold free ends to front and glue. Glue 1 button on top of each folded area of ribbon.

7. Cut 3 (12") lengths from remaining ribbon. Tie each length in bow. Referring to photo, glue 1 bow to top of each ornament. Let dry.

All Boxed Up

These pretty boxes solve a variety of packaging problems. Decorate a large box for storing (or displaying) ornaments or lights, or decorate a small one for presenting homebaked treats.

Materials

For each:
Fabric glue
Sponge paintbrush
Decoupage medium
Black paint pen

For lights box:
Green spray paint
10"-diameter round papier-mâché box
Fabric scraps: orange, yellow, blue, red

For bird box:
¼ yard red fabric
8"-diameter round papier-mâché box
3 yards 1"-wide black-and-white polka-dot
    grosgrain ribbon
Hot-glue gun and glue sticks

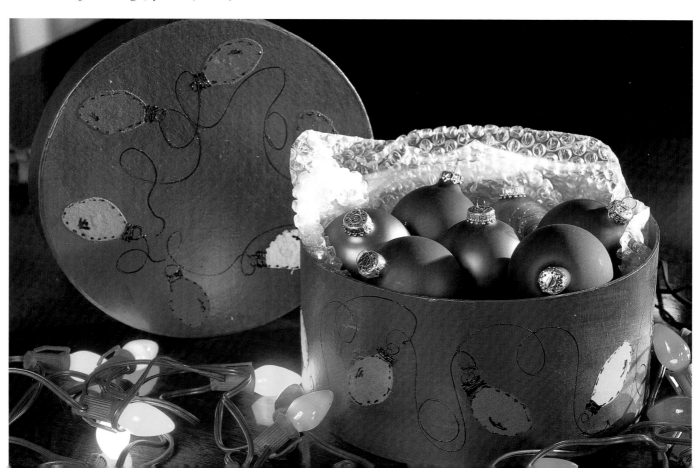

Instructions for lights box

Spray-paint box and lid green. Let dry. Trace light-bulb pattern onto fabric scraps and cut total of 15 light bulbs. Glue light blubs around bottom of box and on top of lid (see photo at left). Let dry. Using sponge brush, apply 1 coat of decoupage medium to entire box. Let dry. Use black paint pen to add string and details to light blubs. Let dry.

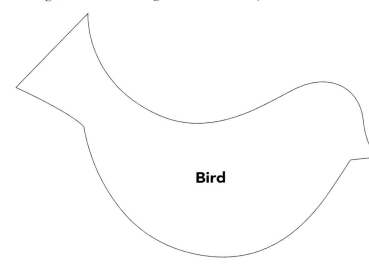

Bird

Instructions for bird box

1. Trace bird pattern onto fabric and cut 3; reverse pattern and cut 3 more. Remove lid from box and set aside. Referring to photo above, use fabric glue to attach birds around bottom of box. Let dry.

2. Using sponge brush, apply 1 coat of decoupage medium to entire box. Let dry. Add details to birds with black paint pen. Let dry.

3. Cut 2 (9½") lengths from ribbon. Cross ribbon lengths on top of lid. Use hot-glue gun to glue ends of ribbons to sides of lid. Cut 1 (26") length from remaining ribbon. Hot-glue ribbon around sides of lid. Tie remaining ribbon in multilooped bow (see General Instructions on page 6) and hot-glue to center of lid.

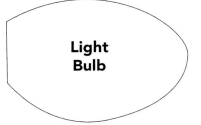

Light Bulb

*W*onderful
W ine Bags

It's all in the presentation, and a bottle of wine has never seemed more special than when wrapped in elegant velvet or funky burlap.

Materials

For each:
Thread to match fabric
Ruler
Bottle of wine
For velvet bag:
2 (7½" x 18") pieces velvet
18" length satin cording
For burlap bag:
Fun Foam scrap
Foam-core board or thick cardboard scrap
Tacky glue
Waxed paper
Metallic acrylic paint in desired color
Paper plate
2 (7½" x 18") pieces burlap
Paper towels
18" length sheer ribbon

Instructions for velvet bag

1. With right sides facing and raw edges aligned, stitch velvet pieces together along both long edges and 1 short end, using ½" seam allowances.
2. To square off bottom of bag, align 1 side seam with bottom seam. Referring to Diagram, measure and mark 1½" from tip of corner along each edge; draw line to connect marks. Stitch across line. Repeat for remaining corner. Turn bag right side out.

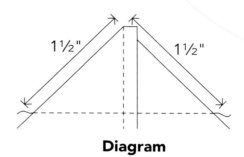

1½"   1½"

Diagram

3. To hem top of bag, fold top raw edge under ½". Fold under again and stitch in place.
4. Place wine in bag. Referring to photo, loosely tie top of bag with satin cording.

Instructions for burlap bag

1. To make stamp, trace swirl pattern onto Fun Foam scrap. Cut out. Glue foam swirl onto foam-core board or cardboard scrap. Let dry.
2. Cover work surface with waxed paper. Pour puddle of paint onto paper plate. Dip stamp into paint and then stamp design onto 1 side of each burlap piece. (Practice stamping on paper towels first to determine correct amount of paint and pressure.) Let dry.
3. Stitch burlap pieces together as in steps 1–3 of instructions for velvet bag. Place wine in bag. Referring to photo, tie top of bag with sheer ribbon.

Swirl

Pyramid Wrap

This pyramid is a unique way to present perfume, a watch, or any special small gift. Taylor the fabric to the holiday or the occasion you are celebrating.

Materials

Ruler
18" square each posterboard, paper-backed fusible web, and fabric
Hole punch
Craft glue
1⅓ yards trim
Mechanical pencil
Tissue paper to coordinate with fabric
Small gift (approximately 6" square or less)
28" length each of 2 different ribbons
Tassels

Instructions

1. Use ruler to draw 16" equilateral triangle on 1 side of posterboard square. Turn posterboard over. Set aside. Aligning edges, press fusible web square onto wrong side of fabric square. Remove paper backing. Aligning edges, fuse fabric square to blank side of posterboard square. Cut out triangle along marked lines.

2. Punch 1 hole in each tip of triangle. Glue trim along edges of triangle. Let dry. Place triangle fabric side down. From 1 tip of triangle, measure and mark 8" along 1 edge. Using ruler and metal tip of mechanical pencil, score straight line across triangle (see Diagram). Repeat with remaining 2 tips of triangle.

3. Loosely wrap tissue paper around gift. Place gift in center of triangle. Holding both ribbons as one, lace ribbons through 2 holes. Pull points of triangle up and run both ends of ribbons through third hole. Loop tassle through holes. Tie ribbons in bow and trim ends.

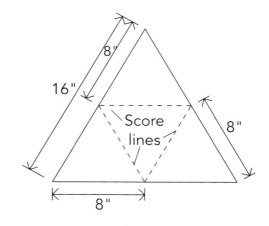

Diagram

Packaging *Pouches*

These stamped pouches are perfect for wrapping gifts of unusual size or shape, such as a small clock or a decorative knickknack.

Materials

Fun Foam scraps
Foam-core board or cardboard scraps
Tacky glue
Waxed paper
Acrylic paints in desired colors
Paper plates
White medium-weight woven fabric*
Paper towels
Pencil with eraser
Desired gift
1 yard ribbon
Note: Fabric yardage will depend on size of gift. When gift is placed in center of fabric square, fabric should pull up over gift and extend approximately 6" above gift.

Instructions

1. Trace desired patterns onto Fun Foam scraps and cut out. For each shape, cut 1 (2") square from foam core or cardboard. To make stamps, glue each foam shape onto 1 (2") foam-core square.

2. Cover work surface with waxed paper. Place fabric square faceup on waxed paper. Pour puddle of each color of paint onto separate paper plates. Dip 1 foam stamp into desired color of paint and stamp fabric. (Practice stamping on paper towels first to determine correct amount of paint and pressure.) Repeat as desired to complete design. To make dots, use pencil eraser dipped into paint. Let dry.

3. Place stamped fabric facedown. Center gift in fabric square. Pull fabric up around gift and cinch at top of gift. Tie ribbon in bow to secure.

Cut out shaded areas.

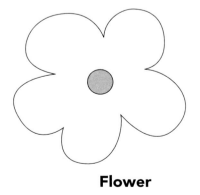

Flower

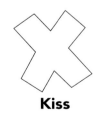

Kiss

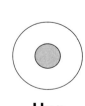

Hug

Heart

Sock It
to the Seasons

Celebrate the holidays right down to your toes. The appliqués on these socks pin on for easy removal when laundering.

Materials

For each pair:
Paper-backed fusible web
Fabric glue
2 bar pins
Pair of purchased socks with cuffs in desired color

For star socks:
Blue fabric scraps
Red felt scraps
5 (2") lengths each ⅛"-wide satin ribbons: blue, red

For jack-o'-lantern socks:
Fabric scraps: orange, black, light green, dark green
Felt scraps: black, green

For bunny socks:
White fabric scraps
Purple felt scraps
Brown thread
Hand-sewing needle
2 (6") lengths ⅛"-wide pink satin ribbons
2 (½") white pom-poms

Instructions

1. **For star socks,** trace star pattern 2 times onto paper side of fusible web. Roughly cut out shapes. Press star shapes onto wrong side of blue fabric scraps. Cut out shapes along pattern lines. Fuse star shapes to red felt scraps. Trim felt, leaving approximate ⅛" margin around fabric appliqués.

2. For each star, glue 1 end each of 5 lengths of ribbon to back of star (see photo). Let dry. Glue 1 bar pin to center back of each star. Let dry. Pin 1 star decoration to cuff of each sock.

3. **For jack-o'-lantern socks,** transfer pumpkin, face, leaf, and stem patterns 2 times each to paper side of fusible web. Roughly cut out shapes. Press shapes onto wrong side of fabric scraps as follows: pumpkins onto orange, face details onto black, leaves onto light green, and stems onto dark green. Cut out shapes along pattern lines. Referring to photo, fuse stems, pumpkins, and face details to black felt scraps. Trim felt, leaving approximate ⅛" margin around fabric appliqués.

4. Glue 1 bar pin to center back of each jack-o'-lantern. Let dry. Pin 1 jack-o'-lantern decoration to cuff of each sock.

5. **For bunny socks,** trace bunny pattern 2 times to paper side of fusible web. Roughly cut out shapes. Press bunny shapes onto wrong side of white fabric scraps. Cut out shapes along pattern lines. Fuse bunny shapes to purple felt scraps. Trim felt, leaving approximate ⅛" margin around fabric appliqués.

6. Using brown thread, sew tiny X on each bunny for eye, as shown on pattern. Tie each pink ribbon length in tiny bow. Referring to photo, glue 1 bow and 1 pom-pom tail in place on each bunny. Glue 1 bar pin to center back of each bunny. Let dry. Pin 1 bunny decoration to cuff of each sock.

Star

Jack-o'-lantern

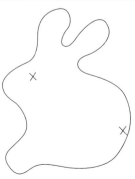

Bunny

*S*heer Happiness Cards

Mixed media make these cards extraspecial. Filmy sheer fabric gives softness to the paper; ribbon and machine embroidery add an element of romance.

Materials

For each:
Pinking shears
Glue stick
For black-and-white photo card:
8½" x 11" piece card stock in desired color
5" x 8" piece sheer organza with selvage along 1 short edge
4 black photo mounting corners
3½" x 5" black-and-white photo
Fine-tip permanent black marker
Hole punch
8" length 1½"-wide black-and-white wire-edged ribbon
Envelope to fit 5½" x 8½" card
For heart card:
6" x 11" piece card stock in desired color
Piece red paper
7" square sheer organza
Contrasting thread in 2 different colors
Embroidery scissors
Envelope to fit 5½" x 6" card

Instructions for black-and-white photo card

1. Fold card stock in half widthwise. Using pinking shears, trim organza along long edges and short edge without selvage. Referring to photo and using glue stick, glue selvage edge of organza to top edge of folded card stock.
2. Lift organza and use photo mounting corners to attach photo to front of card as desired. (If photo mounting corners are not self-adhesive, apply glue to backs.) Using black marker, write message below photo. Replace organza.
3. Punch 2 holes, ½" apart and ¾" above photo, at top center of card. Thread ribbon through holes and tie in knot at front of card. Trim ribbon ends in V. Place card in envelope.

Instructions for heart card

1. Fold card stock in half widthwise. Trace heart onto red paper and cut out with pinking shears. Center organza on top of heart and secure, using glue stick.
2. Referring to photo and using small zigzag stitches with desired colors of thread, stitch on top of organza just inside heart. Repeat to stitch 3 more hearts in graduating sizes. Stitch designs inside hearts if desired, referring to photo for inspiration. Using embroidery scissors, trim organza close to first stitched heart.
3. Glue red heart to center front of card. Let dry. Place card in envelope.

Heart

Happy Mother's Day
We love you

Holiday Table

Celebrate the arrival of January first with New Year's Eve Confetti Tablecloth (page 62). Show your true colors when you set the table with the patriotic Old Glory Place Mat (page 70). Autumn Leaf Table Runner (page 76) creates just the right mood for a Thanksgiving feast.

New Year's Eve
Confetti Tablecloth

This cloth will set a ticker-tape tone for your New Year's festivities! And believe it or not, it's entirely no-sew!

Materials

Heavy-duty paper-backed fusible web scraps
Fabrics: lining scraps in jewel tones, 2½ yards 45"-wide sheer white, gold lamé scraps
Pressing paper or aluminium foil
Heavy-duty paper-backed fusible web tape: ⅜"-wide, ⅝"-wide
Metallic pearl cotton: gold, silver
5½ yards ⅝"-wide sheer white striped ribbon

⅜"-wide fusible tape strips

8"
8"
8"
8"
8"
8"
8"

45"

Diagram

Instructions

Note: Finished tablecloth is 45" square.

1. Press fusible web scraps onto wrong side of lining fabric scraps. Remove paper backing. Referring to photo, cut lining fabric scraps into roughly 1" pieces.

2. Cut sheer fabric into 2 (45") squares. Cover work surface with pressing paper or aluminum foil. (If possible, work on 45" or larger surface.) Spread 1 square of sheer fabric on work surface. Scatter lining fabric pieces, web side down, on sheer fabric square. When satisfied with arrangement, beginning at 1 corner, fuse lining fabric pieces to sheer fabric square.

3. Referring to Diagram and beginning at 1 corner, press strips of ⅜"-wide fusible tape diagonally across tablecloth, spacing strips 8" apart. Beginning in adjacent corner, repeat to press fusible tape strips diagonally in opposite direction to create checkerboard pattern. Remove paper backing.

4. Cut each color of metallic pearl cotton into 6" to 36" lengths. Separate lengths into individual strands. Referring to photo, scatter strands on embellished sheer fabric square. When satisfied with arrangement, stack remaining 45" sheer fabric square on top of embellished square and align edges. Place pressing paper or aluminum foil over fabric squares. Beginning in center, iron toward sides to join fabric squares and to secure threads in place.

5. Press ⅝"-wide fusible tape onto wrong side of sheer ribbon. Remove paper backing. Beginning in 1 corner, align outside long edge of ribbon with edge of fabric. Fuse ribbon in place along edge of fabric, trimming ribbon at corner. Continue in this manner to fuse ribbon to remaining edges of tablecloth, overlapping ribbon at corners.

6. To launder, wash by hand and hang to dry.

Tabletop
Easter Pots

Embellish terra-cotta pots with whimsical appliqués and then fill them with bright spring plants for a table decoration that the Easter Bunny will love.

Materials (for 3 small and 3 large pots)

Paper-backed fusible web scraps

Fabric scraps

Clay pots: 3 (3"-diameter x 4"-tall) and 3 (6½"-diameter x 5"-tall)

White pom-poms: 5 (¼"), 1 (½")

Craft glue

Instructions

1. Press fusible web scraps onto wrong side of fabric scraps.

2. Referring to photo for colors and page 66 for patterns, on paper side of fabric scraps, trace following: **For small bunny pot,** trace 5 small bunnies. **For small egg pot,** trace 5 small eggs and 1 small pot grass. **For small flowerpot,** trace 2 flowers and 2 flower stems. **For large bunny pot,** trace 1 large bunny, 1 large pot grass, 1 large pot grass reversed, and 2 small eggs. **For large egg pot,** trace 6 large eggs and desired number of egg stripes, rickrack, and polka dots. **For large flower pot,** trace 5 flowers and 5 flower stems. **For each,** cut out shapes along pattern lines. Remove paper backing. Referring to photo, fuse shapes to sides of pots.

3. For small bunny pot, referring to photo, glue 1 (¼") pom-pom to bottom of each small bunny. **For large bunny pot,** referring to photo, glue ½" pom-pom to back of large bunny. Let dry.

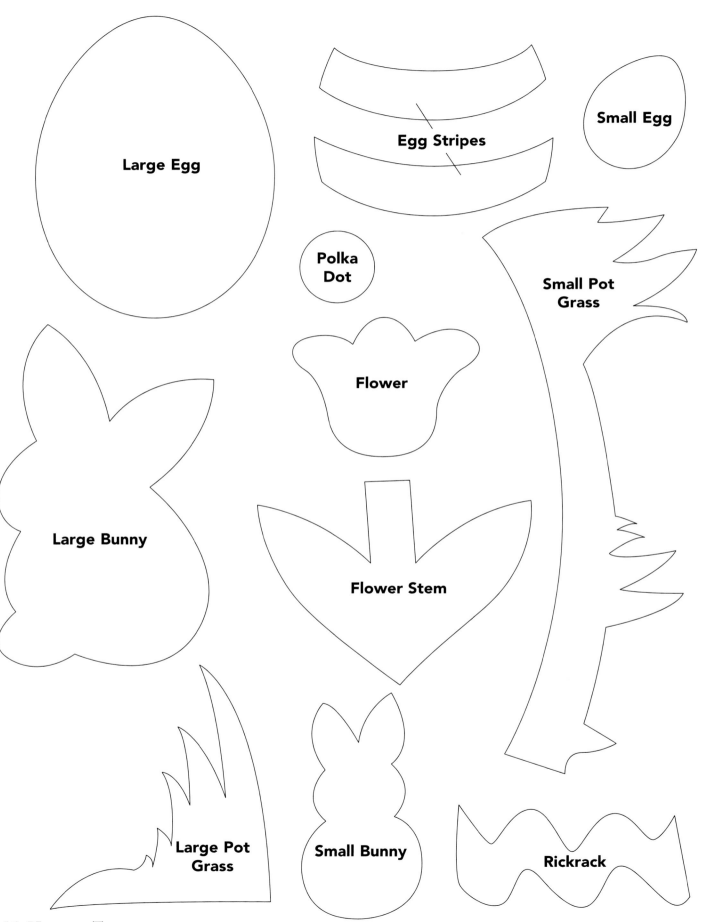

Large Egg

Egg Stripes

Small Egg

Polka Dot

Small Pot Grass

Flower

Large Bunny

Flower Stem

Large Pot Grass

Small Bunny

Rickrack

Reverse Collage
Holiday Plates

Plates are versatile decorating elements. Display them in a cupboard, on plate stands, or on the wall.

Materials

For each:
Black dimensional paint
Fabric glue
Paintbrush
Plain clear glass plate
White acrylic paint
Paper plate
1½" square piece sponge
Paper towel
Clear acrylic spray sealer
For bunny plate:
Fabric scraps: light blue checked, pink
Dimensional paints: white, green
For chick plate:
Fabric scraps: yellow, pink, light blue
Dimensional paints: green, white, orange
For holly plate:
Fabric scraps: green, red
For snowman plate:
Fabric scraps: white, red-and-black print, red solid,
    black, orange

Instructions

1. **For each,** transfer desired patterns to right side of fabric scraps (see photos on page 67 and at right). Cut out shapes along pattern lines.

2. **For bunny plate,** paint eye and nose with black. Let dry. Apply glue to right sides of bunny and squiggles. Turn plate over. Referring to photo on page 67, glue bunny facedown in center of plate; glue squiggles around rim of plate. Still working from back of plate, paint dots around bunny, using white dimensional paint. Let dry. Then paint green dots along outline of squiggles and green grass blades under bunny. Let dry.

3. **For chick plate,** glue fabric zigzag to right side of fabric stripe; then glue fabric stripe to right side of fabric egg. Let dry. Referring to photo on page 67, paint green dots along edges of zigzag and stripe. Let dry. Then paint dots along edges of egg, using white dimensional paint. Let dry. Paint eye on each chick with black. Let dry. Apply glue to right side of egg and each chick. Turn plate over. Referring to photo on page 67, glue egg facedown

in center of plate; glue chicks around rim of plate. Still working from back of plate, paint orange beak and black legs on each chick; then paint green grass blades under chicks. Let dry.

4. **For holly plate,** paint veins along center of each holly leaf with black. Let dry. Apply glue to right side of each holly leaf and berry. Turn plate over. Referring to photo below, glue holly leaves and berries around rim of plate. Let dry.

5. **For snowman plate,** glue pieces to snowman in following order: arms, buttons, scarf, nose, and hat. Let dry. Paint eyes and mouth with black. Let dry. Apply glue to right side of snowman. Turn plate over. Referring to photo below, glue snowman facedown in center of plate. Let dry.

6. **For each,** pour puddle of white acrylic paint on paper plate. Wet sponge and squeeze out excess water. Dip sponge into white paint. Press sponge on paper towel to remove excess paint. Lightly sponge-paint back of plate (see photo). Let dry. Spray back of plate with 1 coat of acrylic sealer. Let dry.

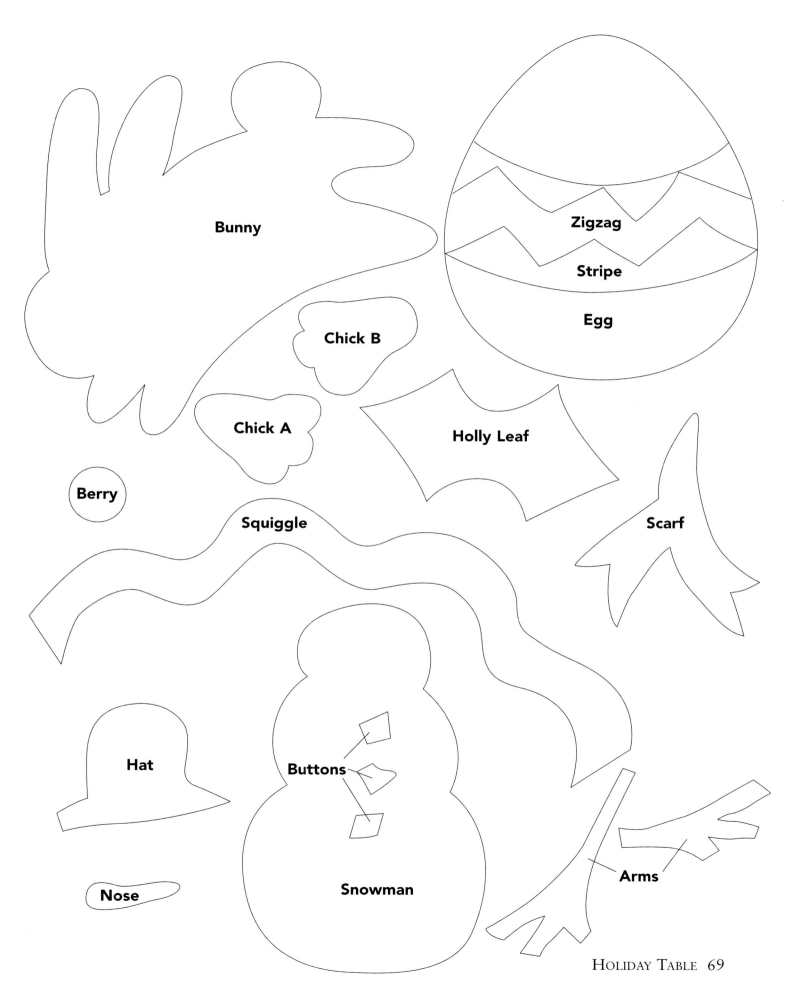

Bunny

Zigzag

Stripe

Egg

Chick B

Chick A

Holly Leaf

Berry

Squiggle

Scarf

Hat

Buttons

Nose

Snowman

Arms

Old Glory
Place Mat

Add patriotic style to your Independence Day table with a set of stars-and-stripes place mats. Jumbo rickrack lends a playful quality and makes construction simple.

Materials (for 1 place mat)

Fabrics: ½ yard white, ¼ yard blue
3½ yards wide red rickrack
7" x 12" piece paper-backed fusible web
Thread: red, white
7" x 13" piece tear-away stabilizer (optional)
14" x 20" piece batting

Instructions

1. From white fabric, cut 1 (7" x 12") piece, 1 (13") square, and 1 (13" x 19") piece. From blue fabric, cut 1 (7" x 13") piece. From rickrack, cut 7 (18") lengths.

2. Press paper-backed fusible web onto wrong side of 7" x 12" white fabric piece. Trace 3 stars onto paper side of fabric. Cut out shapes along pattern lines. Remove paper backing.

3. Beginning ¾" from top and bottom edges, position rickrack lengths on 13" white fabric square, evenly spacing rickrack lengths and aligning curves. Using red thread, stitch down center of each rickrack length. Tim ends of rickrack even with white square.

4. With right sides facing, align 1 long edge of blue fabric piece with left side edge of 13" white square (see photo). Stitch together, using ½" seam allowance. Press seam toward blue fabric.

5. Position stars on blue fabric, approximately 1" from top and bottom edges and ¾" from right side seam. Fuse stars in place. Using white thread, machine satin-stitch raw edges of stars. (If fabric is lightweight, you may need to put tear-away stabilizer behind stars before satin-stitching.)

6. Layer batting, place-mat top (right side up), and 13" x 19" white piece (right side down). Pin together and stitch, using ½" seam allowance and leaving 5" opening along bottom edge for turning. Turn right side out and slipstitch opening closed. Press place mat.

Star

Candy Corn
Table Accessories

This lighthearted place setting is a tribute to the most fun Halloween candy of all time.

Materials

For each:
Paper-backed fusible web scraps
Fabric scraps: white, yellow, orange
For 1 place mat:
¾"-wide paper-backed fusible web tape
1 yard 1"-wide black-and-white plaid ribbon
Purchased black place mat
1¼ yards small orange rickrack
Fabric glue
For 1 napkin ring:
14" length 1"-wide black-and-white plaid ribbon
Purchased napkin

Instructions for place mat

1. Press fusible web scraps onto wrong side of fabric scraps. On paper side of scraps, trace 6 candy corn shapes onto white fabric, 6 yellow stripes onto yellow fabric, and 6 orange stripes onto orange fabric. Cut out shapes along pattern lines. Remove paper backing.

2. Press fusible web tape onto wrong side of ribbon length. Remove paper backing. Measure width and length of place mat. Cut 1 piece of ribbon equal to each measurement and 2 pieces of rickrack equal to length.

3. Referring to photo, fuse long ribbon piece to 1 long edge of place mat and remaining ribbon piece to 1 side edge. Glue 1 rickrack piece to top and bottom edges of horizontal ribbon length. Let dry.

4. Referring to photo, fuse white candy-corn shapes to place mat, positioning randomly along ribbon lengths. With bottom edges aligned, position 1 yellow stripe piece on each candy-corn shape and fuse in place. With top edge of yellow stripe and bottom edge of orange stripe aligned, position 1 orange stripe piece on each candy-corn shape and fuse in place.

Instructions for napkin ring

1. Press fusible web scraps onto wrong side of fabric scraps. On paper side of scraps, trace 2 candy corn shapes onto white fabric, 2 yellow stripes onto yellow fabric, and 2 orange stripes onto orange fabric. Cut out shapes along pattern lines. Remove paper backing.

2. With web sides facing, sandwich center of ribbon length between 2 white candy-corn shapes. Fuse candy-corn shapes together, adhering ribbon between them.

3. With bottom edges aligned, position 1 yellow stripe piece on 1 candy-corn shape and fuse in place. With top edge of yellow stripe and bottom edge of orange stripe aligned, position 1 orange stripe piece on candy-corn shape and fuse in place. Repeat to fuse yellow and orange stripes on opposite side of candy corn. Tie ribbon napkin ring around napkin.

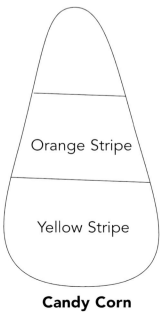

Candy Corn

Turkey
Pot Holder

No room gets more use during the Thanksgiving holidays than the kitchen, so why not give it a bit of seasonal flair? The appliqué featured on this pot holder also works well on a dish towel or a place mat.

Materials
Paper-backed fusible web scraps
Fabric scraps: burgundy solid, beige print,
    2 different burgundy prints
Purchased beige terry-cloth pot holder
Embroidery needle
Embroidery floss: burgundy, dark brown, yellow

Instructions
1. Press fusible web scraps onto wrong side of fabric scraps. On paper side of fabric scraps, trace 1 body on burgundy solid, 5 feathers on beige print, and 3 feathers each on burgundy prints. Cut out shapes along pattern lines. Remove paper backing.
2. Referring to photo for arrangement, position feathers in center of pot holder, overlapping edges. Fuse feathers in place. Position body on top of feathers and fuse in place.
3. Using embroidery needle and burgundy floss, make running stitches along edges of body and feathers. Referring to photo and using brown floss, straightstitch turkey legs (see General Instructions, page 7) and satin-stitch eyes. Using yellow floss, satin-stitch beak and make 1 tiny stitch in each eye for highlight.

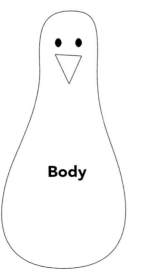

Body

Feather

Autumn Leaf
Table Runner

Place this rustic cloth down the center of a table, a buffet, or an island and then adorn it with a variety of gourds, nuts, and wheat sheaves.

Materials

Heavy-duty paper-backed fusible web scraps
Fabric scraps: gold, yellow, brown
18" x 40" piece burlap

Instructions

Press fusible web scraps onto wrong side of fabric scraps. Trace leaf pattern onto paper side of fabric scraps approximately 21 times. Cut out shapes along pattern lines. Remove paper backing. Referring to photo, scatter leaves along edges of burlap piece, positioning leaves approximately 2" to 3" from edges of fabric. Fuse leaves in place. Fringe approximately 1" along each edge of burlap. When needed, spot-clean table runner with soap and water.

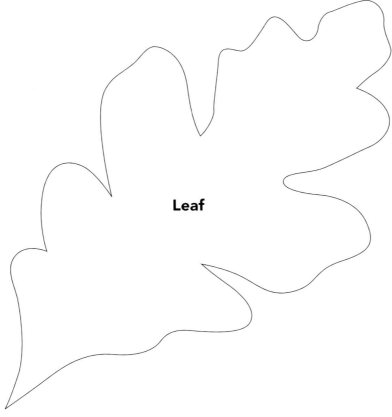

Leaf

Harvest
and Bread Cloth

*...reads taste even better when served
...his cozy basket and cloth.*

Materials

For both:
Paper-backed fusible web scraps
Fabric scraps in 3 different autumn colors

For basket:
Thin 100%-cotton batting scraps
⅛" hole punch
Raffia
Purchased basket with handle
Hot-glue gun and glue sticks

For bread cloth:
Ivory cotton dish towel or napkin*
*Note: If unable to find ivory dish towel, purchase 100%-cotton white dish towel and tea-dye it by soaking it in tea bath for 5 minutes. Rinse dish towel thoroughly and let dry.

Instructions for basket

1. Press fusible web scraps onto wrong side of fabric scraps. Remove paper backing. Cut fabric scraps and batting scraps each into approximately 4" squares. Sandwich 1 batting scrap between 2 matching fabric scraps and fuse. Repeat with remaining fabric and batting scraps.

2. Trace desired number of acorns, acorn caps, and leaves in desired shapes onto fused fabric squares. Cut out shapes along pattern lines.

3. Punch 2 holes approximately ¼" apart in top of each leaf. Lace leaves onto 1 length of raffia. Add more raffia lengths to laced leaf length. Referring to photo and holding all raffia lengths as 1, tie raffia around basket rim. If necessary, hot-glue raffia in place on basket. Then hot-glue acorns to handle of basket.

Instructions for bread cloth

Press fusible web scraps onto wrong sides of fabric scraps. Trace 1 leaf A, 2 acorns, and 2 acorn caps onto paper side of fabric scraps. (Acorn caps and bodies should be cut from different fabrics.) Cut out shapes along pattern lines. Remove paper backing. Referring to photo, fuse shapes to 1 corner of dish towel. To launder, wash by hand.

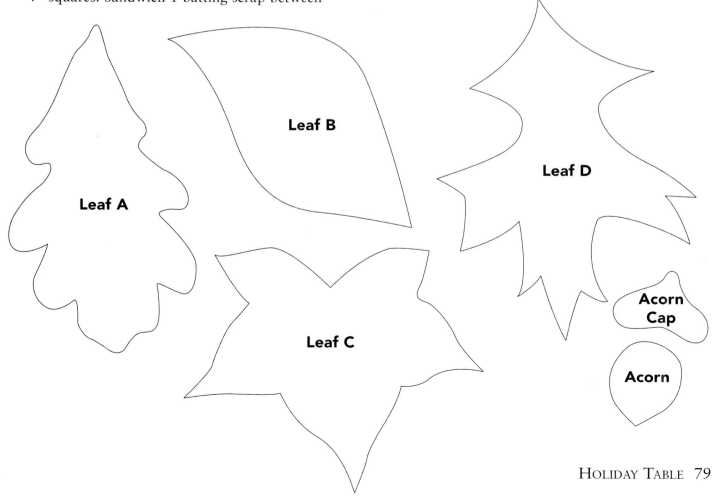

Leaf B

Leaf A

Leaf D

Leaf C

Acorn Cap

Acorn

O Christmas
Tree

Who would ever guess that these terrific trees are actually stacked clay pots? Colorful buttons and country gingham accents give them a warm, folksy charm.

Materials (for 1 large tree and 1 small tree)

Green enamel spray paint
Clay pots: 1 (10"), 2 (8"), 2 (6"), 2 (4")
$^5/_{16}$" dowels: 1 (17") length, 1 (22") length
Measuring tape
$^1/_4$ yard green plaid fabric
Craft glue
Clothespins
Green thread
Stuffing
Hot-glue gun and glue sticks
Approximately 60 various buttons: red round, red
   heart, wooden, Christmas novelty shapes
8 yards $^1/_8$"-wide green satin ribbon

Instructions

1. Spray-paint clay pots and dowels green. Let dry.
2. Measure width and circumference of lip of each pot. Add $^1/_4$" to each width measurement and $^1/_2$" to each length measurement. Using these measurements, cut fabric strips. Fringe $^1/_4$" along long edges of each fabric strip. Using craft glue, glue fabric strips to lip of each corresponding pot. Let dry. (Use clothespins to hold fabric strips in place while glue dries.)
3. Transfer star pattern to remaining fabric and cut 4. With wrong sides facing and raw edges aligned, stitch 2 star shapes together, using $^1/_4$" seam allowance and leaving $^3/_4$" open at bottom. Slightly fringe edges of stitched star. Repeat with remaining fabric star shapes. Stuff each star through opening. Insert 1 end of 1 dowel into 1 star through opening. Using combination of craft glue and hot glue, glue fabric closed around dowel. Repeat with remaining star and dowel.
4. Turn 10" pot upside down. Referring to photo, stack 1 (8"), 1 (6"), and 1 (4") pot on top of 10" pot; then stack remaining 8", 6", and 4" pots. Insert 22" dowel through holes in pots of large stacked tree and 17" dowel through holes in pots of small tree.
5. Using combination of craft glue and hot glue, glue buttons to sides of pots as desired. For each ribbon-embellished button, cut 2$^1/_2$" length of ribbon, thread ribbon through holes in button, and tie ribbon in knot at front of button. For ribbon-and-button garland along fabric strips on large tree, cut 1 length of ribbon for each strip, measuring length of strip and adding 3". Thread buttons onto ribbon, spacing as desired (see photo). Tie ribbon around corresponding strip. Apply dot of hot glue under each button to hold garland in place.

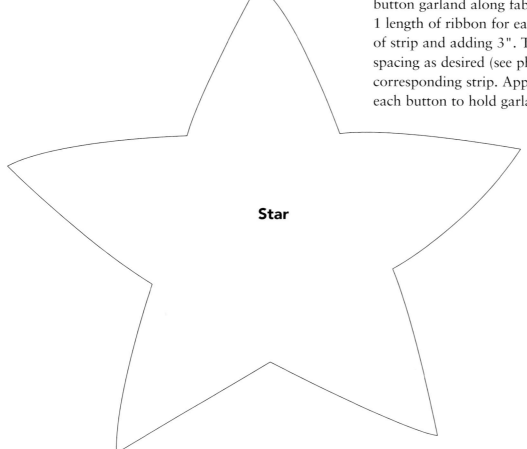

Star

Pretty Package
Place Mat

The simple style of this holiday place mat allows it to complement any Christmas china pattern you may have.

Materials (for 1 place mat)

$7/8$"-wide paper-backed fusible web tape
2 (15" x 20") pieces plaid fabric
2 (13" x 18") pieces heavyweight nonwoven
   interfacing
$1\frac{1}{2}$ yards 1"-wide grosgrain ribbon
Needle and thread

Instructions

1. With edges aligned and working on wrong side, press web tape along all edges of fabric pieces. Do not remove paper backing. Center 1 interfacing piece on wrong side of each fabric piece. For each, fold fabric over edges of interfacing; press. Unfold. Remove paper backing from web tape. Refold and fuse edges of fabric to interfacing.

2. From ribbon, cut 1 (13") length and 1 (20") length. Press web tape onto 1 side of each ribbon length. Remove paper backing. Referring to photo, position ribbon lengths on right side of 1 fabric piece, allowing 1" of ribbon to extend beyond edges of fabric piece at each end. Fuse each ribbon in place. Fold ends of ribbons to wrong side of fabric piece and fuse in place. From remaining ribbon, tie bow. Trim ends. Using needle and thread, stitch bow at ribbon intersection.

3. Place each fabric piece facedown. With edges aligned, press web tape onto wrong side of fabric pieces along all edges. Remove paper backing. With wrong sides facing and edges aligned, fuse fabric pieces together. When needed, spot-clean place mat with soap and water.

Velvet Topiary

When decorating for Christmas, keep these words in mind: tasteful, easy, and inexpensive. This topiary meets all three criteria. Choose velvet and ribbons to coordinate with your holiday color scheme.

Materials (for 1 topiary)

5"-diameter ball topiary form
String
Straight pins
Tissue paper
¼ yard green velvet
Craft glue
1¼ yards green velvet cording
Hot-glue gun and glue sticks
Red ribbon roses: 7 large, 10 small
5"-diameter concrete or terra-cotta pot
Serrated knife (optional)
Florist's foam (optional)
Spanish moss
2 yards each 2 different red-and-white wire-edged
    ribbons

Instructions

1. To make pattern for covering ball, cut 2 pieces of string, each equal in length to circumference of topiary ball. Find and mark center of each string. Referring to Diagram, pin strings at marks to top of ball. Wrap strings around ball so that they divide ball into quarters. Pin ends of strings to ball at bottom next to stick.

2. Trace 1 quarter section onto tissue paper. Cut out pattern. Remove strings. Using pattern, trace 4 quarter pieces onto wrong side of velvet and cut out. Leaving ½" margin, apply craft glue to center of each velvet piece on wrong side. Place velvet pieces on topiary ball, matching seams. On wrong side, apply glue to margins of each velvet piece; ease fabric to fit curve of ball. Let dry.

3. Cut 2 pieces of velvet cording, each equal in length to circumference of topiary ball. Position velvet cording lengths on topiary ball to cover fabric seams (see photo). Hot-glue velvet cording in place. Referring to photo, hot-glue ribbon roses to topiary ball as desired.

4. Fit topiary base into pot, trimming if necessary with knife. If base does not fit snuggly in pot, use wedges of florist's foam to secure. Hot-glue Spanish moss to top of foam base. Holding ribbon lengths together, tie ribbons in bow around topiary stick. Use dab of hot-glue to hold ribbons in place if necessary.

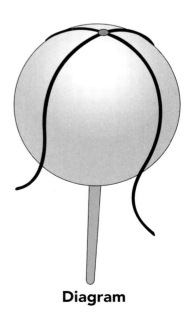

Diagram

Elegant
Envelope Tablecloth

Stitch a linen hankie to each corner of a purchased tablecloth to create "envelopes" into which you can tuck small gifts. Instruct each guest seated at the table to look inside the pocket next to him or her for a special surprise.

Materials

4 embroidered handkerchiefs
Thread to match handkerchiefs and ribbon
Hand-sewing needle
4 satin ribbon flowers
Purchased tablecloth
Straight pins
8 yards 1"-wide sheer ribbon
28 satin ribbon roses

Instructions

1. To make handkerchief envelopes, fold 3 corners of 1 handkerchief to center and press fold lines (see photo). Using matching thread, slipstitch points of corners together. Hand-stitch 1 ribbon flower at intersection. Repeat with remaining handkerchiefs.

2. Place tablecloth on table. Measure "drop" of tablecloth. (Drop of tablecloth is fabric that hangs off edge of table.) Referring to Diagram, at 1 corner of tablecloth, measure determined drop from 2 adjacent sides. Insert pin where measurements intersect. Place point of handkerchief envelope at mark and arrange so that handkerchief is equidistant from edges. Slipstitch handkerchief to tablecloth. In same manner, slipstitch remaining handkerchief envelopes to remaining corners of tablecloth.

3. Cut ribbon into 4 equal lengths. Fold 1 length of ribbon in half. Using thread to match ribbon, make running stitches across width of ribbon at center fold and pull to gather ribbon. Wrap thread around gathered area twice and take 2 stitches to secure. Locate center of bottom edge of 1 handkerchief envelope. Place gathered area of ribbon 1" below center and whipstitch to tablecloth. With thread still attached, stitch through bottom of 1 ribbon rose; stitch rose in place on top of gathered area of ribbon. Push needle to back of tablecloth, tie off thread and trim excess.

Measure 5" (or desired distance) from first gathered area on ribbon and gather another area as above. Whipstitch in place at bottom corner of handkerchief and finish as above. Continue in same manner around both sides of handkerchief. At top corners, fold 2 loops in ribbon and gather across entire area, leaving 5" tail of ribbon. Repeat to attach ribbon to remaining 3 corners of tablecloth.

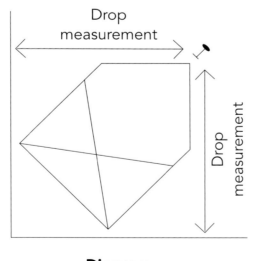

Diagram

Holidays at Home

$\mathcal{T}$he Easter Bunny will feel right at home when he sees your Spring Chick Pillowcase (page 98). Greet trick-or-treaters, neighbors, and the mailman with the boo-tiful Spirited Mailbox Cover (page 105). Snowman Tree Topper (page 113) will produce squeals of delight.

*H*eavenly Hearts

*These puffy pillows will tug on your heartstrings.
They immediately bring a sense of romance
wherever you hang them.*

Pearl-Edged Heart

Lace-Trimmed Heart

Diagonal-Ribbon Heart

Materials

For each:
⅓ yard fabric
Straight pins
Thread to match fabric
Hand-sewing needle
Stuffing

For pearl-edged heart:
2 yards 1⅜"-wide sheer ribbon
1 yard pearl piping

For diagonal-ribbon heart:
2 yards 1⅝"-wide sheer ribbon

For lace-trimmed heart:
1 yard ½"-wide pearl-trimmed lace

Instructions

1. **For each,** trace heart pattern onto fabric and cut 2.

2. **For pearl-edged heart,** cut sheer ribbon in half. With 1 cut end of each ribbon aligned with edges of fabric, pin 1 end of each ribbon length to right side of 1 fabric heart where indicated by dots on pattern. With lip of pearl piping aligned with edges of fabric, pin piping around same fabric heart; trim excess. From remaining piping, clip off individual pearls and tack as desired to right side of same fabric heart. With right sides facing, raw edges aligned, and hanger loop to inside, stitch hearts together, using ½" seam allowance and leaving opening for turning.

3. **For diagonal-ribbon heart,** from sheer ribbon, cut 1 (18") length and 2 (27") lengths. With cut ends of ribbon aligned with edges of fabric, pin 18" length to right side of 1 fabric heart where indicated by dots on pattern and 1 (27") length to upper left curve of heart; then pin remaining 27" length to lower right side of heart (see photo). With right sides facing, raw edges aligned, and hanger loop and side ribbons to inside, stitch hearts together, using ½" seam allowance and leaving opening for turning.

4. **For lace-trimmed heart,** cut 1 (18") length, 1 (4") length, 1 (7½") length, and 1 (6") length from pearl-trimmed lace. With cut ends of lace aligned with edges of fabric and pearls facedown, pin 18" length to right side of 1 fabric heart where indicated by dots on pattern. With cut ends of lace aligned with edges of fabric and pearls faceup, pin 4" length to right side of same fabric heart across top right edge, 7½" length across center of heart, and 6" length across lower left edge of heart (see photo). With right sides facing, raw edges aligned, and hanger loop to inside, stitch hearts together, using ½" seam allowance and leaving opening for turning.

5. **For each,** turn heart right side out. Stuff. Slipstitch opening closed. **For pearl-edged heart,** tie free ends of hanger ribbon in bow approximately 9" above top of heart. Trim ends of ribbon. **For diagonal-ribbon heart,** tie free ends of ribbon in bow at front of heart. Trim ends of ribbon.

Hanger dots

Heart

Luck-of-the-Irish
Dish Towel

Even if your pay for washing the dishes isn't a pot of gold, you'll still feel a wee bit lucky when drying dishes with this towel.

Materials

Paper-backed fusible web scraps
Green plaid fabric scraps
Purchased green dish towel
Gold dimensional fabric paint

Instructions

Press fusible web scraps onto wrong side of fabric scraps. Trace patterns onto paper side of fabric scraps. Cut out shapes along pattern lines. Remove paper backing. Referring to photo, center and fuse shapes to 1 short end of dish towel. Outline shapes with gold dimensional paint. Let dry at least 24 hours before use. To launder, wash in gentle cycle and dry on low temperature.

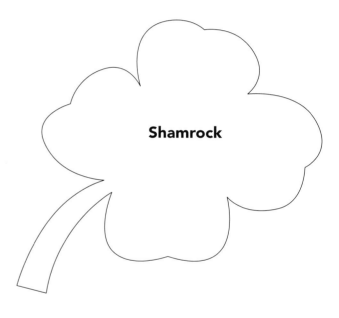

Shamrock

*E*aster
Banner

As colorful as a garden of spring flowers, this happy banner shows your enthusiasm for the holiday.

Materials

¾"- or ⅞"-wide heavyweight paper-backed
    fusible web tape
Fabrics: 20" x 24" piece white duck cloth and
    18" x 24" piece Easter print, each cut out with
    pinking shears; 11" x 13" piece and scrap pink
    solid; 6½" x 8" piece pink check; 7½" x 8"
    piece pink stripe; 7" x 11" piece white; scraps
    for basket, eggs, flowers, and stems
Pinking shears
Disappearing-ink fabric marker
Ruler
Heavyweight paper-backed fusible web
Dimensional fabric paints: light blue, white, gray
26" length ⅜"-diameter wooden dowel
1⅓ yards white braided cording
2¼ yards ⅝"-wide lavender wire-edged ribbon,
    cut in half

Instructions

1. Cut 24" length of fusible web tape. Press tape length along 1 long edge of duck cloth. Remove paper backing. To make casing, fold edge under 2" and fuse to back of duck cloth.

2. Using disappearing-ink marker and ruler,

measure and mark 12¼" x 18" rectangle in center of 18" x 24" Easter print piece. Using pinking shears, cut out marked interior rectangle to create fabric frame. Cut 4 (24") lengths and 4 (18") lengths of fusible web tape. Referring to Diagram

on page 96, press tape lengths along interior and exterior edges on wrong side of fabric frame. Remove paper backing. Set aside.

3. From fusible web, cut 1 (11" x 13") piece, 1 (6½" x 8") piece, and 1 (7½" x 8") piece.

Press fusible web pieces onto wrong side of corresponding pink solid, pink check, and pink stripe fabric pieces. Remove paper backing. Referring to photo, place pink solid piece 2½" from top and left side edge on front of duck cloth piece. With

1 (8") edge at top, position pink stripe next to pink solid, overlapping side edges slightly; position pink check beneath pink stripe, overlapping top and side edges slightly (see photo on pages 94 and 95). Fuse pieces in place. With edges aligned, fuse fabric frame on front of duck cloth piece to cover raw edges of pink fabrics.

4. Press fusible web onto wrong side of white fabric piece and fabric scraps. Referring to photo for number and colors, trace patterns onto paper side of corresponding fabric pieces. Cut out shapes along pattern lines. Remove paper backing.

Referring to photo for positioning, fuse shapes to front of banner.

5. Referring to photo and using dimensional fabric paints, write "Happy Easter!" on pink stripe rectangle with blue; outline flowers, draw veins along centers of leaves, and draw basket handle with white; and outline bunny and add details with gray. Let dry.

6. Insert dowel through casing. For hanger, tie 1 end of cording in knot at each end of dowel. Tie 1 length of ribbon in bow at each end of dowel.

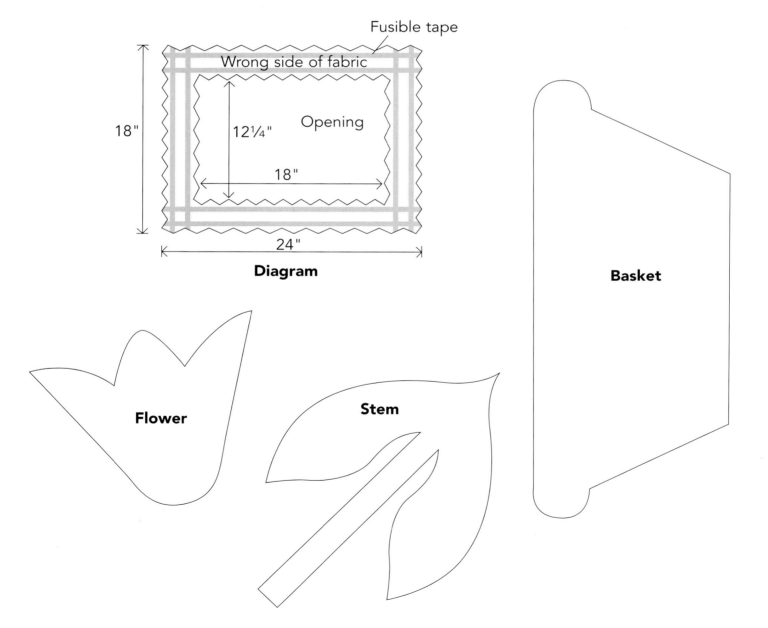

Fusible tape

Wrong side of fabric

18"

12¼"

Opening

18"

24"

Diagram

Flower

Stem

Basket

Egg

Green lines are painted lines.

Bunny

Spring Chick
Pillowcase

Turn egg-shaped appliqués into colorful chicks to adorn pillowcases, sheets, or other fabric projects.

Materials

Straight pins
41" length each green rickrack: medium-width, jumbo-width
Purchased white pillowcase
Embroidery floss: bright green, orange, brown
Embroidery needle
Paper-backed fusible web scraps
Pastel fabric scraps
White thread

Instructions

1. Pin medium-width rickrack to seam line of hem of pillowcase. Pin jumbo-width rickrack approximately 1" below medium-width rickrack. Using 3 strands of bright green floss and embroidery needle, use alternating slanting straightstitches to stitch rickrack in place.

2. Press paper-backed fusible web scraps to wrong side of fabric scraps. Trace desired number of chicks onto paper side of fabric scraps. Cut out shapes along pattern lines. Remove paper backing. Referring to photo, fuse shapes to pillowcase slightly above medium-width rickrack. Using white thread and medium-width zigzag, stitch along edges of facric shapes.

3. Using 3 strands of floss, stitch chick beaks with orange and stitch chick eyes and legs with brown.

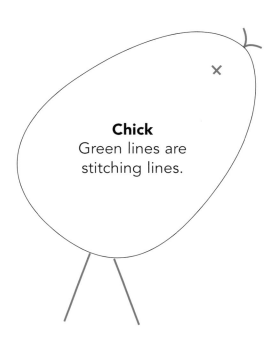

Chick
Green lines are stitching lines.

Patriotic Picnic Basket

A plain wicker basket will be a hit at your Independence Day picnic. Construction of the padded lid is surprisingly easy.

Materials

Purchased picnic basket with hinged lid
Cardboard piece (slightly larger than basket lid)
Sponge paintbrush
Fabric glue
½ yard thin batting
Fabrics: ½ yard red check, blue scraps
Masking tape
White thread
Hand-sewing needle
Hot-glue gun and glue sticks
Paper-backed fusible web scraps
Blue dimensional fabric paint

Instructions

1. Place basket upside down on cardboard and trace lid. Cut out cardboard lid. Using sponge brush, apply 1 coat of fabric glue to 1 side of cardboard lid. Center cardboard lid, glue side down, on batting. Let dry. Trim batting, following outline of lid. Place cardboard lid, batting side down, on wrong side of red check fabric. Cut out around lid, leaving 2" margin. Pull excess fabric to back of cardboard lid and tape fabric in place.

2. Measure circumference of basket lid. From remaining red check fabric, cut 4"-wide strip equal in length to twice circumference of lid. (Piece strips, if necessary, to achieve necessary length.) Fold 4"-wide fabric strip in half lengthwise. Run gathering stitches ¾" and 1¼" from long raw edge. Pull threads to gather ruffle.

3. Hot-glue ruffle to rim of basket lid (see photo). Fold raw edge of ruffle to top of lid and hot-glue in place. Hot-glue fabric-covered cardboard lid to top of basket lid, covering raw edge of ruffle.

4. Press fusible web onto wrong side of blue fabric scraps. Trace desired number of stars onto paper side of fabric scraps. Cut out shapes along fabric lines. Remove paper backing. Fuse stars to top of padded basket lid.

5. Outline stars with dimensional fabric paint. Let dry. Paint dots along gathers of ruffle. Let dry.

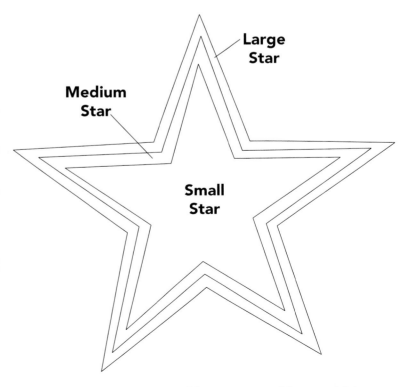

Large Star

Medium Star

Small Star

Haunted
Hangers

Loop these lightweight banners over a post, a doorknob, or anywhere you want to welcome friendly goblins.

Materials

For each:

Awl or ice pick

5¾" x 20" piece foam-core board, with 1 side gray*

Wire cutters

Wire clothes hanger

Pliers

Fabric glue

For jack-o'-lantern door hanger:

Fabric scraps: orange gingham, orange solid, yellow solid, tiny black-and-white check

Silk leaves

1 yard 1"-wide orange ribbon

For witch door hanger:

Fabric scraps: black solid, tiny black-and-white check, green solid, and orange gingham

Felt scraps: gray, burgundy, black

2 (15-mm) wiggle eyes

⅔ yard small black rickrack

16" length ⅛"-wide black satin ribbon

*Note: If foam-core board does not have 1 gray side, spray-paint 1 side gray. Let paint dry.

Instructions

1. For each, use awl or ice pick to punch 2 holes in 1 short end of foam-core board piece, positioning holes approximately ½" from short end and ½" from each side edge. Use wire cutters to cut 16" length from clothes hanger. Working from white side of foam-core board, insert 1 end of clothes-hanger length into each hole in foam-core board.

Use pliers to bend ends of clothes hanger up (see photo).

2. For jack-o'-lantern door hanger, draw 1 (5¼") diameter and 2 (3½"-diameter) circles on orange gingham and 2 (4¼"-diameter) circles on orange solid. Referring to photo for colors, trace 5 desired faces onto right side of orange solid, yellow solid, or black-and-white check fabrics. Cut out shapes along pattern lines.

3. Referring to photo, position circles on foam-core board in following order, overlapping slightly: 5¼" on bottom, 1 (4¼"), 1 (3½"), remaining 4¼", and remaining 3½" on top. When satisfied with placement, glue in place. Glue 1 desired face on each circle. Glue individual silk leaves as desired to top of each jack-o'-lantern. Let dry. Tie orange ribbon in bow around 1 edge of wire hanger.

4. For witch door hanger, on right side of fabrics, trace 1 dress (see page 104) and 1 hat onto black solid; 1 cape (see page 104), 1 reversed cape, and 1 hat brim onto black-and-white check; 1 face onto green solid; and 1 small star, 1 medium star, and 1 large star (see page 104) onto orange gingham.

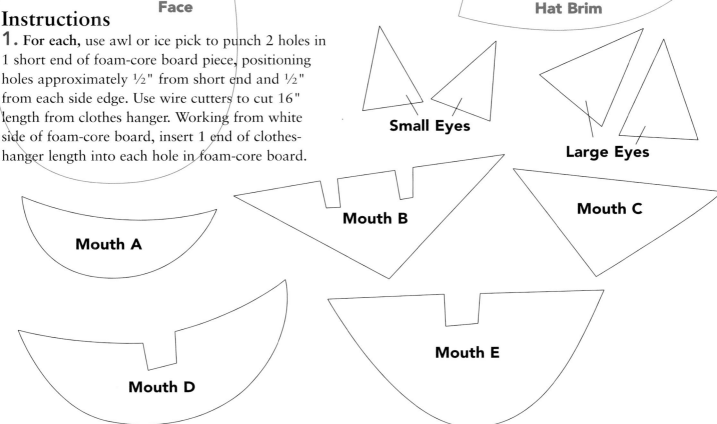

Hat

Face

Hat Brim

Small Eyes

Large Eyes

Mouth B

Mouth C

Mouth A

Mouth D

Mouth E

Then trace 1 nose onto gray felt, 1 mouth onto burgundy felt, and 1 hair and 1 reversed hair onto black felt. Cut out shapes along pattern lines.

5. Referring to photo on page 102, glue shapes in place on foam-core board. Glue wiggle eyes in place on witch's face. Glue rickrack along each inside edge of cape and across center of hat brim. Tie black ribbon in bow and glue to neck of witch. Let dry.

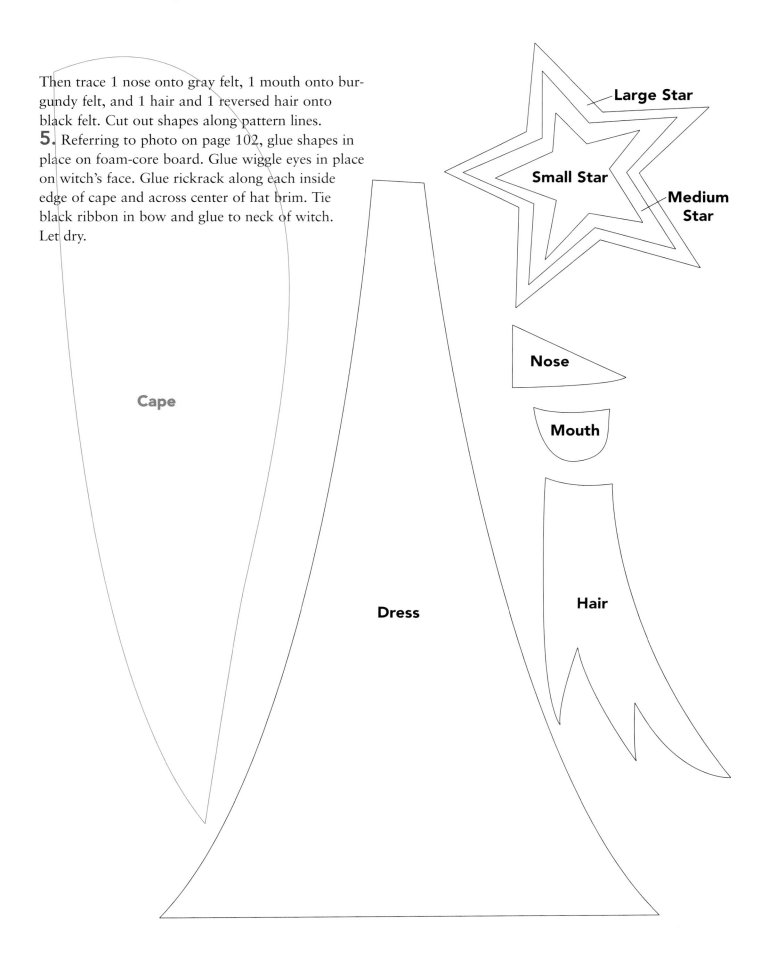

Large Star

Small Star

Medium Star

Cape

Dress

Nose

Mouth

Hair

Spirited
Mailbox Cover

A mailbox provides a wonderful decorating opportunity. This quick-and-easy banner is full of mischief and adds a good measure of Halloween fun to your streetscape.

Materials

Heavyweight paper-backed fusible web
Duckcloth: 12" x 18" piece white; 6" x 12" piece black; 5" x 9" piece yellow; 18" x 40" piece orange, cut out with pinking shears
Pinking shears
E-6000 glue
Wiggle eyes: 4 (7-mm), 4 (18-mm)
Dimensional fabric paints: white, red
2¾ yards 1"-wide orange grosgrain ribbon

Instructions

1. From fusible web, cut 1 (12" x 18") piece, 1 (6" x 12") piece, and 1 (5" x 9") piece. Press fusible web pieces onto wrong side of corresponding duckcloth pieces. On paper side of fabrics, trace ghost onto white duckcloth and cut 2; trace bat onto black duckcloth and cut 2; and trace moon onto yellow duckcloth and cut 2. Cut out shapes along pattern lines. Remove paper backing. Referring to photo, fuse 1 set of shapes to each short end of orange duckcloth piece, positioning bottom edge of each ghost approximately 2" from short edge.

2. Glue 2 (7-mm) wiggle eyes in place on each bat and 2 (18-mm) wiggle eyes in place on each ghost. Let dry. Referring to photo on page 105, use white fabric paint to paint round mouth on each bat and red fabric paint to paint smiling mouth on each ghost. Let dry.

3. From ribbon, cut 2 (21½") lengths and 2 (25½") lengths. Place orange duckcloth piece facedown. Locate area on back where each ghost has been fused to front. Glue 1 end of 1 (21½") ribbon length to back of fabric piece behind each ghost's head so that cut ends of ribbons extend off fabric (see Diagram). Locate area on back where each moon has been fused to front. In same manner, glue 1 end of 1 (25½") ribbon length to back of fabric piece behind center of each moon. Tie mailbox cover to mailbox.

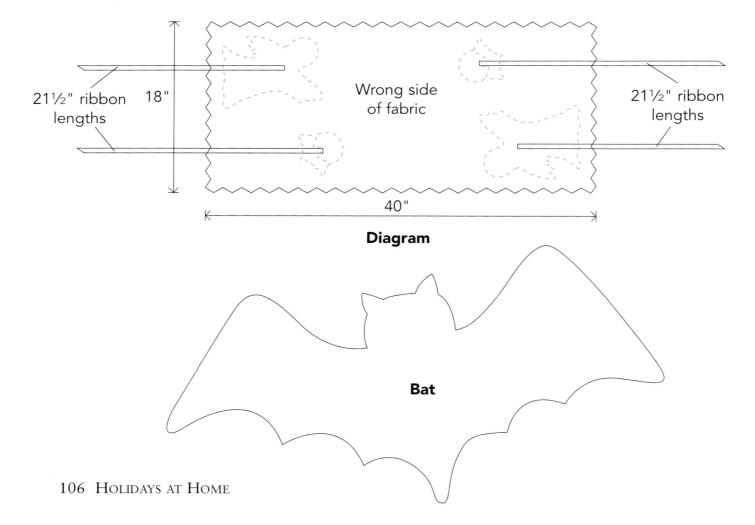

Diagram

21½" ribbon lengths   18"   Wrong side of fabric   21½" ribbon lengths

40"

Bat

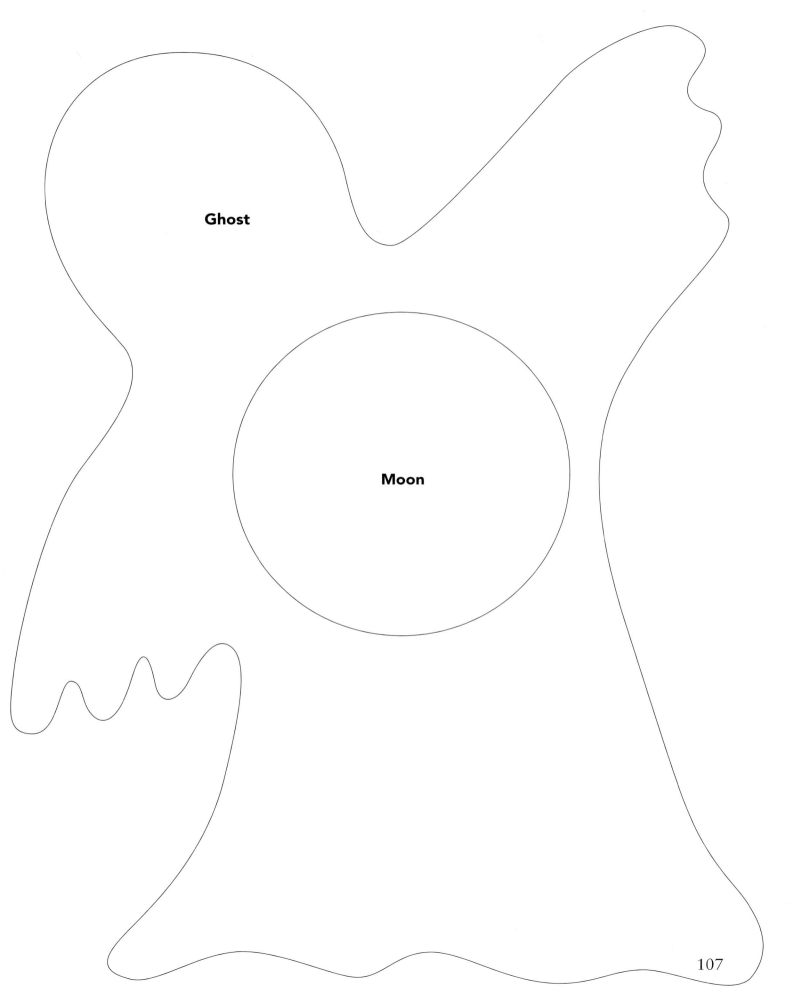

Ghost

Moon

107

Fall
Refrigerator Fun

Why plaster your refrigerator with magnets advertising local realtors or pizza shops when you can decorate it with these cute seasonal magnets? Use other patterns found in this book to make shapes for every holiday.

Materials

For each:
Paper-backed fusible web scraps
Heavyweight watercolor paper
Fabric glue
Sticky-backed magnet strips

For Halloween magnets:
Fabric scraps: orange gingham, tiny black-and-white check, white with black polka dots

Wiggle eyes: 2 (7-mm) for ghost, 2 (12-mm) for bat
1½" length small black rickrack

For Thanksgiving magnets:
Fabric scraps: gold print, green print
Felt scraps: dark brown, cream, black, burgundy
1 (7-mm) wiggle eye for turkey

Instructions

For each set, press fusible web scraps onto wrong side of fabric scraps. **For Thanksgiving magnets,** also fuse web scraps onto felt scraps. **For each set,** referring to photo for colors, trace desired patterns onto paper side of scraps. Cut out shapes along pattern lines. Remove paper backing. Fuse shapes onto watercolor paper. Cut out shapes, following fabric or felt outline. **For Halloween magnets,** use fabric glue to assemble jack-o'-lantern (see photo). Glue wiggle eyes in place on bat and ghost. Glue rickrack mouth in place on bat. Let dry. **For Thanksgiving magnets,** use fabric glue to asemble turkey and acorns. Glue wiggle eyes in place on turkey. **For each set,** adhere strip of magnet to back of each shape.

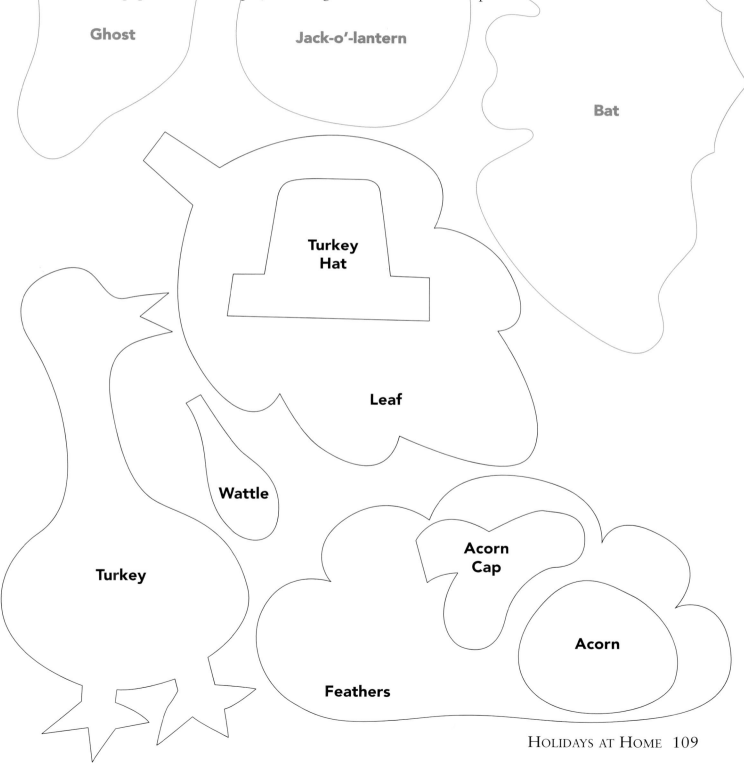

Ghost

Jack-o'-lantern

Bat

Turkey Hat

Leaf

Wattle

Turkey

Acorn Cap

Acorn

Feathers

Falling Leaves
Blanket

As the days turn nippy and darkness sets in earlier, you'll enjoy snuggling under this fleecy autumn throw. Outline the appliqués with fabric paint for a fast finish or satin-stitch around them for a more durable edging.

Materials

Paper-backed fusible web
⅓ yard each 4 different fabrics in autumn colors
Dinner plate
Purchased autumn-color polar fleece blanket
Disappearing-ink fabric marker
Brown dimensional fabric paint

Instructions

1. Trace 20 leaves in desired shapes (see page 112) and 12 acorns and caps each onto paper side of fusible web. Roughly cut out shapes. Press leaves onto wrong side of desired fabrics. Press acorns onto wrong side of 1 fabric; press caps onto wrong side of slightly darker fabric. Cut out shapes along pattern lines. Remove paper backing.

2. Place dinner plate facedown in center of blanket. Using disappearing-ink marker, trace dinner place. Arrange 8 leaves around marked circle. Fuse leaves in place. Arrange 4 acorns and 4 caps in center of leaf circle and fuse in place. Referring to photo, arrange 3 leaves, 2 acorns, and 2 caps in each corner of blanket and fuse in place.

3. Beginning in center of blanket, use fabric paint to outline each leaf, acorn, and cap; add veins down center of each leaf. Let paint dry at least 24 hours before using blanket.

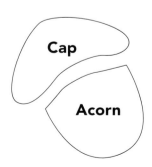

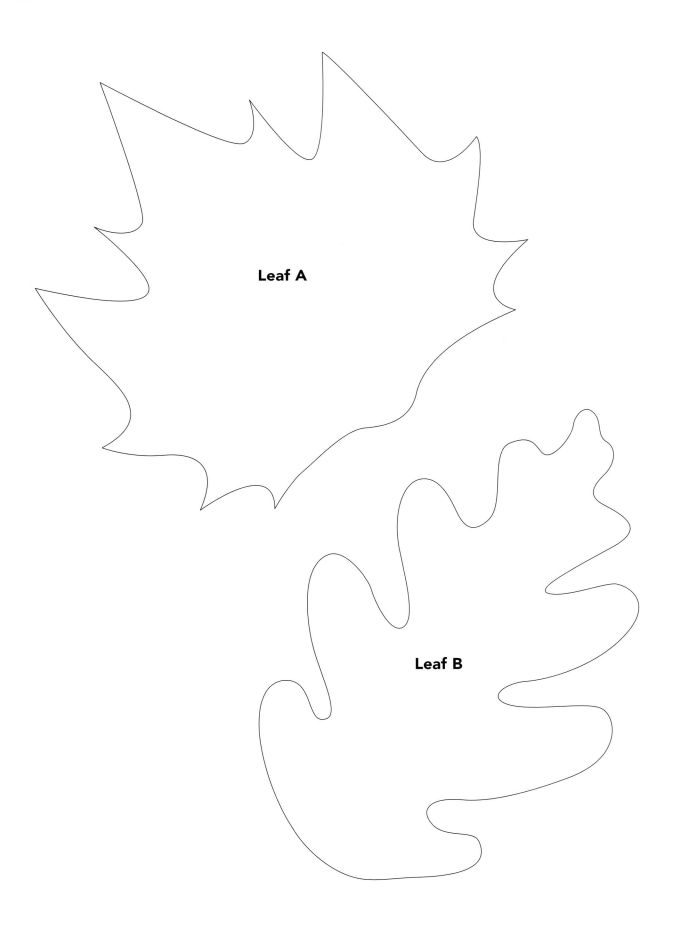

Leaf A

Leaf B

Snowman
Tree Topper

Forget those typical star and angel tree-toppers.
You'll make a fresh and whimsical holiday statement
when you crown your tree with this frosty fellow.

Materials

Felt: 2 (9" x 11") pieces white; yellow, pink, and orange scraps
Fabric glue
Embroidery needle
Embroidery floss: black, orange
White thread
Stuffing
6" length ¾"-wide red-and-white polka-dot grosgrain ribbon
2 (1") red pom-poms
3 (⅜") black buttons
Paper-backed fusible web scrap
Yellow fabric scrap

Instructions

1. Trace snowman onto white felt and cut 2; star onto yellow felt and cut 1; cheek onto pink felt and cut 2; nose onto orange felt and cut 1.

2. Glue pink felt cheeks in place on 1 snowman piece (see photo on page 113). Using embroidery needle and black embroidery floss, make French knots for eyes; make running stitches for snowman's mouth. Roll orange felt nose piece into carrot shape. Use orange embroidery floss to tack felt in place; wrap few additional stitches around entire carrot. Use tiny stitches to tack carrot nose to snowman's face.

3. With wrong sides together and edges aligned, stack snowman pieces. Using white thread and referring to pattern, zigzag snowman pieces together from 1 dot, around top of snowman, to second dot. Lightly stuff head of snowman.

4. To make earmuffs, referring to photo, glue ribbon along top of snowman head, beginning and ending at midcheek point. Trim ribbon ends and tack to snowman head to secure. Tack or glue 1 pom-pom over each end of ribbon.

5. Referring to photo, glue buttons down center front of snowman. Press fusible web onto wrong side of fabric scrap. Trace star onto paper side of fabric scrap. Cut out star slightly inside marked line. Remove paper backing. Center and fuse fabric star to 1 side of yellow felt star. Referring to photo, tack or glue star between snowman hands.

Star

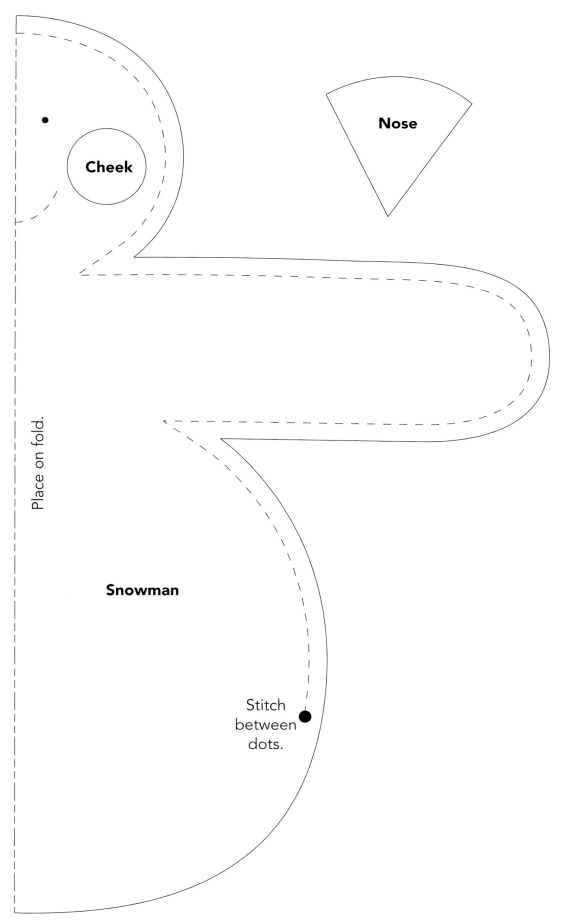

Nose

Cheek

Place on fold.

Snowman

Stitch between dots.

Ribbon *Wreath*

An elegant twist to traditional evergreen, this stunning ribbon wreath looks spectacular over a sofa or a buffet or on the handles of a glass-front cabinet. For outdoor use, make sure to use waterproof ribbons.

Materials

Craft-foam wreath form
Ribbons: 1"- to 2"-wide for wrapping wreath*,
    4 yards desired width wire-edged for 8"-wide
    bow, 16" length desired width for each ribbon
    rose, 15" length 1"-wide for hanger
Straight pins
Hot-glue gun and glue sticks
Florist's wire (optional)
Thread to match ribbon for roses
Hand-sewing needle
Small pinecones
Silk leaves
Artificial berries
*Note: Ribbon yardage will vary acording to diameter of wreath. Wrap wreath form with tape measure to determine amount of ribbon needed.

Instructions

1. Tightly wrap wreath form with 1"- to 2"-wide ribbon, overlapping ribbon slightly (see photo). Secure ribbon at back of wreath with straight pins.
2. To make bow, refer to General Instructions on page 6. Hot-glue or wire bow to top of wreath (see photo).
3. To make ribbon rose, working ¼" from edge of 16" ribbon length, run gathering stitches down right edge and along bottom edge of ribbon (Diagram 1). Pull thread to gather tightly (Diagram 2). Roll gathered ribbon into rosette; tack along bottom edge to secure.
4. Referring to photo, hot-glue ribbon roses, pinecones, silk leaves, and artificial berries to wreath. For hanger, pin cut ends of 15" ribbon length to back of wreath behind bow.

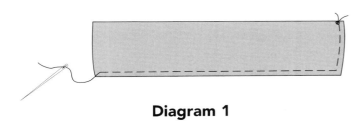

Diagram 1

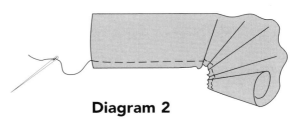

Diagram 2

Greeting Card *Holder*

Looking for a pretty and practical way to display your Christmas cards? This clever box is just the answer.

Materials

Scrap paper for making patterns
Paper-backed fusible web
Fabrics: 7" x 12" piece each 4 different green
    prints; yellow, red, blue, and plaid scraps
Mat board
Craft knife
Ruler and cutting mat
Hot-glue gun and glue sticks
8" x 6" x 3½" wooden crate
Dark green acrylic paint
Sponge paintbrush
12 assorted small white buttons
¼"-wide satin ribbons: green, white
Craft glue

Instructions

1. Trace shapes (see pages 120 and 121) onto scrap paper and cut out patterns. Place tree patterns 1, 2, 3, and 4 facedown on paper side of fusible web and trace. Place 1 star and 10 presents in desired shapes faceup on paper side of fusible web and trace. Roughly cut out each shape. On wrong side of fabrics, press 1 tree shape onto each green fabric piece; star shape onto yellow scrap; and present shapes onto red, blue, and plaid scraps. (For a variety of present shapes, turn web shapes on side or upside down as desired.) Cut out shapes along pattern lines. Remove paper backing.

2. With patterns faceup, tape individual tree patterns together, aligning bases as indicated on patterns to make 1 complete tree pattern. Trace complete tree pattern onto matboard. Using craft knife, ruler, and cutting mat, cut out mat-board tree. Position individual green fabric tree shapes on mat-board tree, aligning outside edges and bases as indicated on patterns. Fuse shapes in place.

3. Fuse remaining shapes to remaining mat board. Using craft knife, ruler, and cutting mat, cut out shapes, following fabric outline. Hot-glue star to top of tree.

4. Paint wooden crate green. Let dry. Hot-glue base of tree to back top edge of wooden crate. Hot-glue buttons to tree as desired.

5. Cut 10 lengths of ribbon equal to width of packages; then tie 10 small bows from remaining ribbon. Using craft glue, glue 1 length of ribbon down center of each package. Glue 1 bow to top of each package (see photo). Let dry. Referring to photo, hot-glue packages to sides of wooden crate, overlapping packages as desired.

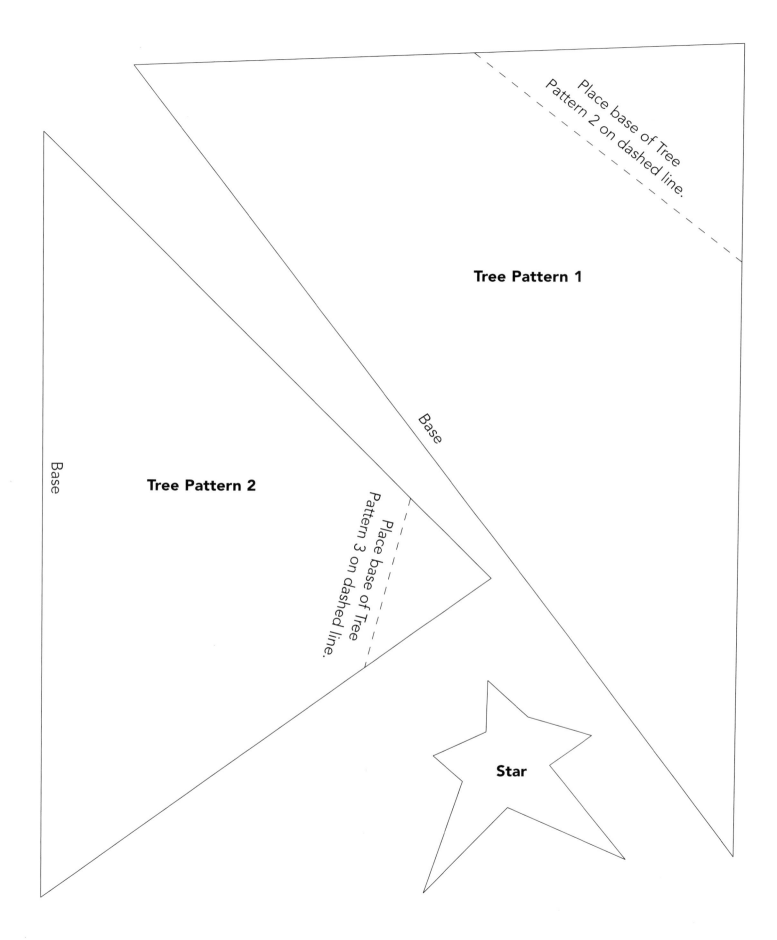

Place base of Tree Pattern 2 on dashed line.

Tree Pattern 1

Base

Base

Tree Pattern 2

Place base of Tree Pattern 3 on dashed line.

Star

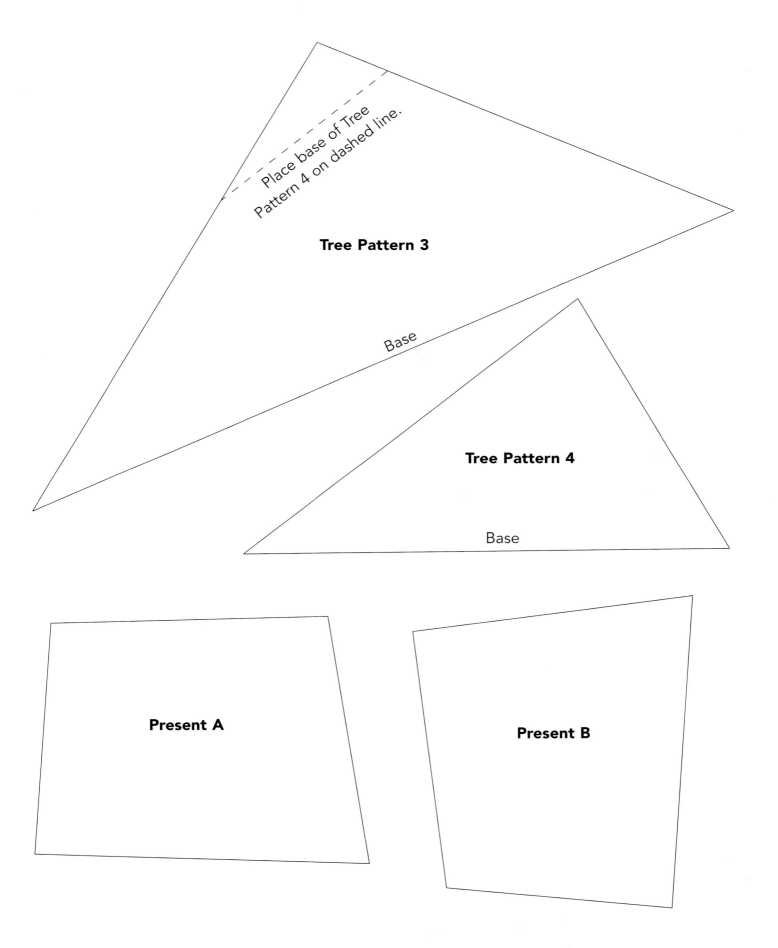

Place base of Tree
Pattern 4 on dashed line.

Tree Pattern 3

Base

Tree Pattern 4

Base

Present A

Present B

Merry Pillow Wraps

As festive as gift-wrapped presents, these faux suede pinafores surround everyday pillows with holiday cheer.

Materials (for both pillow wraps)

45"-wide Ultrasuede: ⅓ yard burgundy, ⅔ yard green
Heavy card stock (such as file folder)
Thread: burgundy, green
7"-diameter 15"-long bolster pillow
Straight pins
Hand-sewing needle
2 (1") star buttons
1 small black bead
12" square pillow

Instructions for Christmas Tree Bolster

1. From burgundy Ultrasuede, cut 1 (11½" x 14") piece and 4 (1" x 12") ties. From green Ultrasuede, cut 1 (14" x 23½") piece.

2. Trace bolster pattern (see page 124) onto card stock and cut out, making template. Place tree template on wrong side of 14" edge of burgundy piece and trace along edge. Cut along marked lines for arc and trees, making sure to cut away all markings.

3. With side edges aligned, place burgundy piece (right side up) on right side of green piece. Using burgundy thread, topstitch burgundy piece to green piece along all cut edges. Trim top edge of green piece to match arc on top edge of burgundy piece.

4. With wrong sides together and cut edges aligned, fold each tie in half lengthwise. Topstitch long edges of each tie. Referring to Diagram 1, place 1 tie at each top corner of burgundy piece; topstitch across 1 end of each tie. Leaving needle in fabric, pivot and stitch diagonally to edge of tie. Again, leaving needle in fabric, pivot and stitch across tie to opposite edge. Pivot again and stitch diagonally to edge of tie, ending stitching where it began.

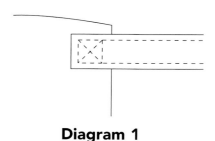

Diagram 1

5. Wrap cover around bolster. Place cover around bolster. Pin 1 tie on each side of cover to correspond with ties on top edge. Using pins, mark placement of star buttons above trees. Remove cover from bolster. Stitch ties in place as in Step 4. Hand-stitch buttons to cover. To secure cover on bolster, make bow with each pair of ties.

Instructions for Reindeer Pillow

1. From remaining burgundy Ultrasuede, cut 1 (12" x 24") piece. From remaining green Ultrasuede, cut 1 (12" x 22") piece and 8 (1" x 11") strips for ties.

2. Trace reindeer pattern (see page 125) onto card stock and cut out, making template. Center reindeer template horizontally on wrong side of 12" x 22" green piece, positioning hooves 1" from 1 (12") edge. Trace along edges. Beginning in center of reindeer, cut out along marked lines, making sure to cut away all markings.

3. With side edges aligned, stack reindeer portion of green piece (right side up) on right side of burgundy piece, overlapping fabrics 10¼" (Diagram 2).

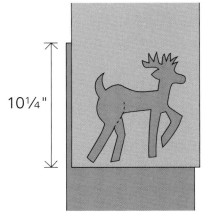

10¼"

Diagram 2

4. Using green thread, topstitch green piece to burgundy piece around reindeer motif. Topstitch bottom and side edges of green piece to burgundy piece. To define reindeer, topstitch across burgundy piece from hind leg to hip, as shown in Diagram 2 on page 123. Referring to pattern for placement, stitch 1 bead to reindeer motif for eye.

5. With wrong sides together and cut edges aligned, fold each tie in half lengthwise. Topstitch long edges of each tie. Place 1 tie at each bottom corner of green piece. From each tie, measure and mark 7¼" up each side edge. Place remaining ties at marks. Referring to Diagram 1 on page 122, stitch ties in place. To determine placement of remaining ties, wrap cover around pillow, overlapping burgundy piece with green piece. Place 1 tie each on green piece in back of cover to correspond with ties on top edge of cover. Remove cover and stitch ties in place as in Step 4 of instructions for Christmas Tree Bolster. Tie cover on pillow.

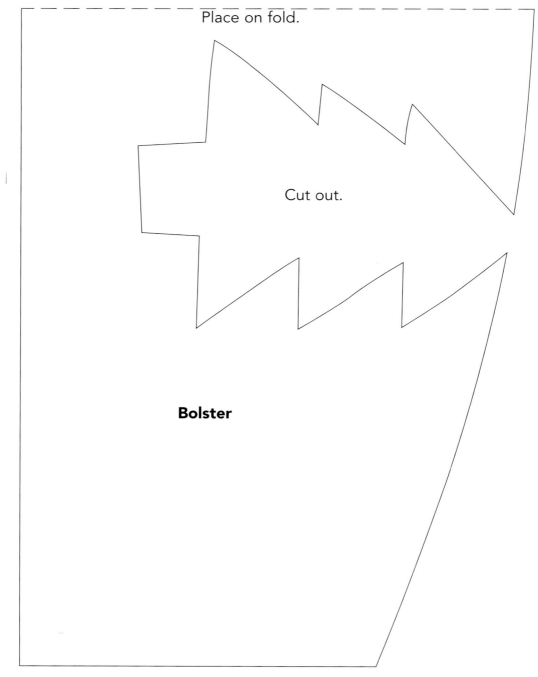

Place on fold.

Cut out.

Bolster

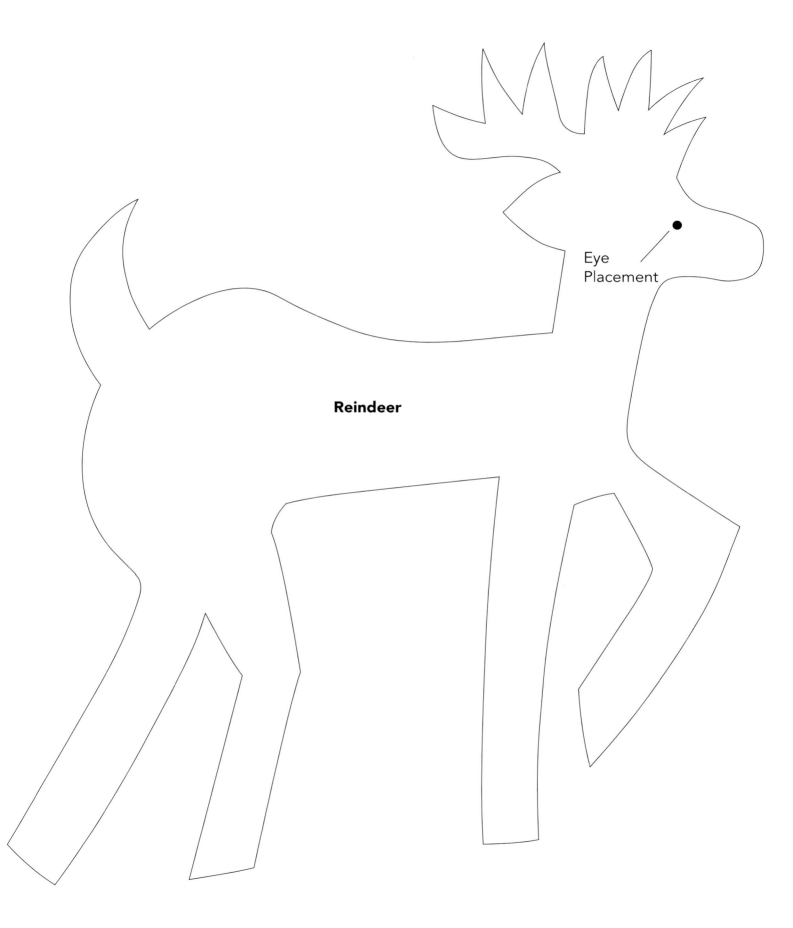

Reindeer

Eye
Placement

Delightful
Dish Towels

Make your kitchen merry and bright by hanging out plaid dish towels that feature two favorite symbols of Christmas.

Materials

For each:
8" x 15" piece paper-backed fusible web
Purchased red-and-white plaid dish towel
Fabric glue

For tree towel:
Green fabric scraps
24 ($\frac{1}{4}$") red pom-poms

For gingerbread man towel:
7" x 10" piece light brown fabric
1$\frac{1}{3}$ yards small white rickrack
8" length $\frac{1}{4}$"-wide red satin ribbon
Thread to match fabric
Hand-sewing needle
5 ($\frac{1}{4}$") black buttons

Instructions

1. **For tree towel,** press fusible web onto wrong side of fabric scraps. Trace 3 trees (see page 128) onto paper side of fabric scraps. Cut out shapes along pattern lines. Remove paper backing. Center 1 tree on 1 short end of towel, 2" from bottom, and fuse in place. Fuse remaining trees on each side, 1$\frac{1}{4}$" from first tree. Glue 8 pom-poms as desired on each tree. Let dry.

2. **For gingerbread man towel,** press fusible web onto wrong side of fabric piece. Trace gingerbread man (see page 128) onto paper side of fabric. Cut out shape along pattern lines. Remove paper backing. Center gingerbread man on 1 short end of towel, 1$\frac{1}{2}$" from bottom, and fuse in place. Beginning and ending between legs, glue rickrack along outline of gingerbread man. Cut 8 (1") pieces from remaining rickrack. Referring to photo, glue 2 (1") rickrack pieces to each wrist and each ankle. Tie ribbon in bow. Glue bow at neck. Let dry. Referring to photo, sew buttons down center of gingerbread man.

3. **For each,** to launder, wash by hand and hang to dry.

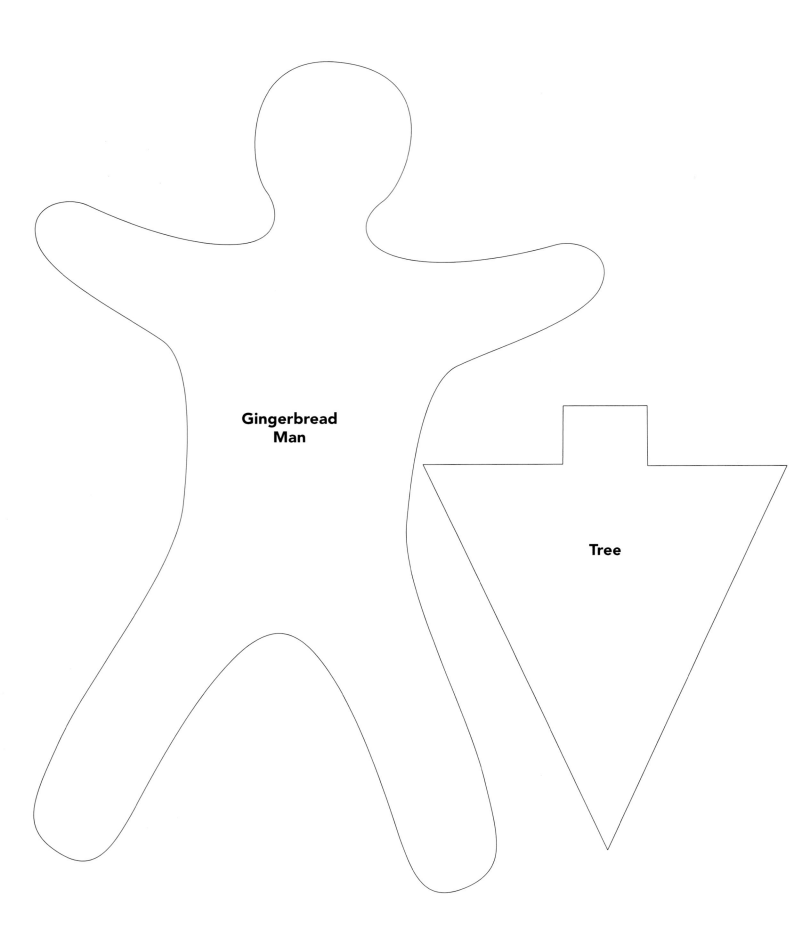

Gingerbread
Man

Tree

Old-fashioned Batting Ornaments

These inexpensive ornaments are ideal for making in multiples. Dunk them in a tea bath, embroider a few stitches, and embellish them with small buttons for a truly homespun touch.

Materials

For each:
Disappearing-ink fabric marker
2 (5") squares needle-punched batting
Straight pins
Red or green embroidery floss
Embroidery needle
Assorted small buttons: green, red, or cream
Coffee or tea, brewed (optional)

Instructions

1. Trace desired pattern onto 1 batting square. Stack and align batting squares, with marked square faceup; pin together. Thread needle with 3 strands of embroidery floss. Referring to General Instructions on page 7, make running stitches approximately ⅛" inside marked pattern line. **For tree ornament,** embellish edges with blanket stitches. **For mitten ornament,** satin-stitch top.

2. For each, cut out along marked pattern line. Knot 1 end of floss for hanger. Stitch through tip of ornament, hiding knot between batting layers. Make loop of floss and secure. Then stitch buttons to ornament as desired.

3. If desired, dip ornament into coffee or tea to stain. Let dry on flat surface.

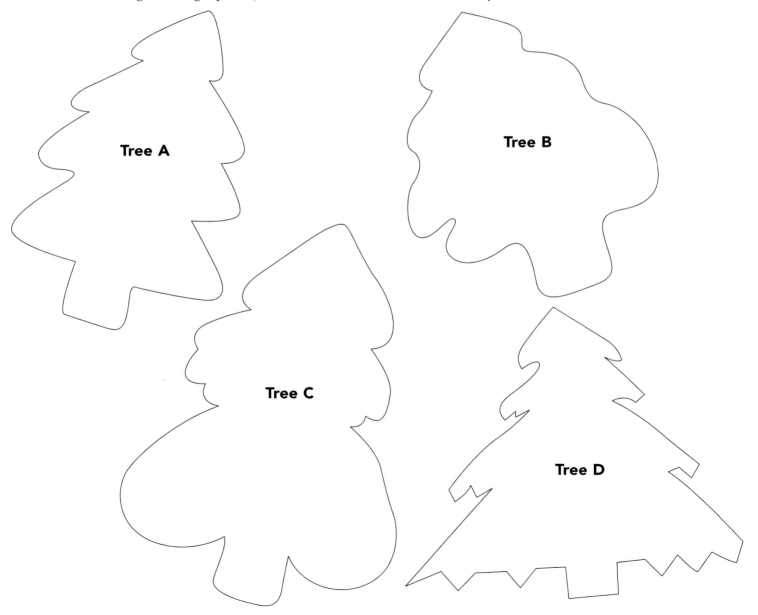

Tree A

Tree B

Tree C

Tree D

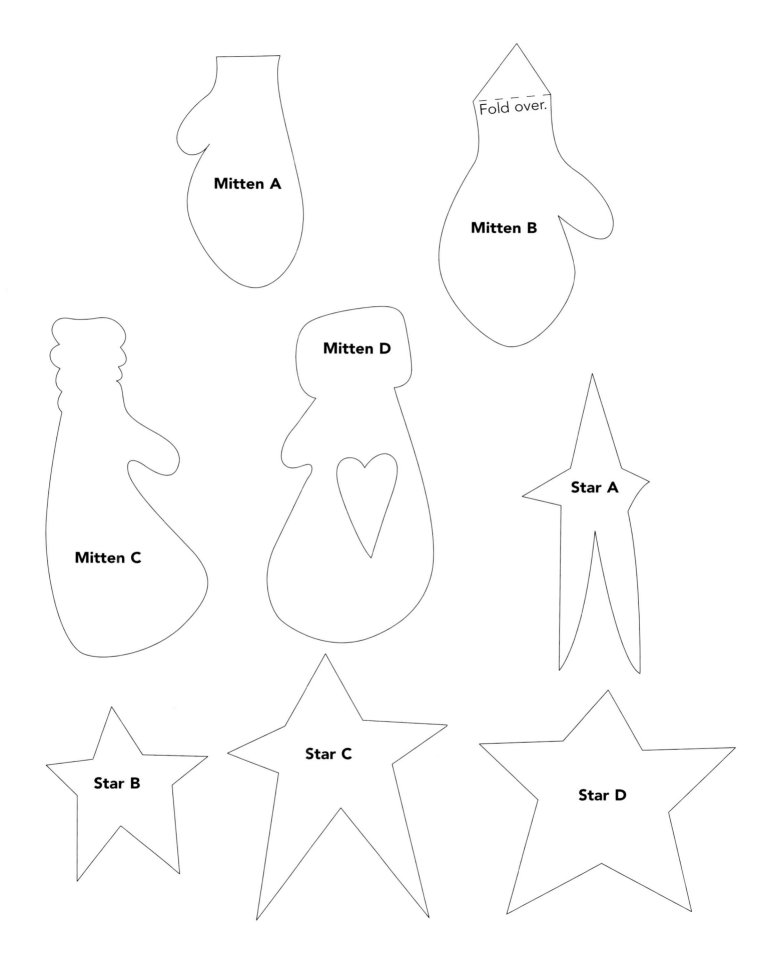

Mitten A

Mitten B

Fold over.

Mitten D

Star A

Mitten C

Star B

Star C

Star D

Jingle Jolly
Stocking

Rich fabrics combine with a playful design to make this stocking a truly unique Christmas accent.

Materials

Tissue paper

Fabrics: ½ yard quilted cotton for stocking, ¼ yard contrasting fabric for cuff, ¾ yard fabric for lining

Disappearing-ink fabric marker

Thread to match fabrics

10" length cording for hanger

Straight pins

Hand-sewing needle

6 (18-mm) jingle bells

Instructions

Note: Seam allowances are ¼" unless otherwise indicated.

1. Trace patterns for cuff and stocking (see pages 134 and 135) onto tissue paper, adding ¼" seam allowance and matching dots on stocking top and bottom to continue pattern; transfer markings. Cut out tissue paper patterns.

2. From stocking fabric, cut 1 stocking; reverse pattern and cut 1 more. From cuff fabric, cut 1 cuff, placing pattern on fold as indicated. From lining fabric, cut 2 stockings and 1 cuff, placing cuff pattern on fold as indicated. Transfer pattern markings.

3. With right sides facing and edges aligned, stitch stocking pieces together along side and bottom edges. Clip curves; turn and press.

4. With right sides facing and raw edges aligned, stitch fabric cuff side seam. Then stitch lining cuff side seam and turn right side out. With right sides together, slip lining cuff inside fabric cuff, aligning side seams and pointed bottom edges. Stitch lining to cuff along pointed bottom edge, pivoting at dots. Clip to dots; trim seam. Turn and press.

5. Pin lining side of cuff to right side of stocking, matching side seams. Baste. Aligning cut ends of cording with raw edges of stocking top, pin cording hanger to heel side of stocking. Baste.

6. Stitch stocking lining pieces together, leaving 5" opening along 1 side seam for turning. Do not turn. With right sides together, slip fabric stocking into lining stocking and pin. Stitch together along top edge, using ⅜" seam allowance. Turn and press. Slipstitch opening closed.

7. Tack 1 jingle bell to each cuff point.

Place this edge on fold.

Cuff

Add ¼" seam allowance to all cut edges.

Add ¼" seam allowance to all cut edges.

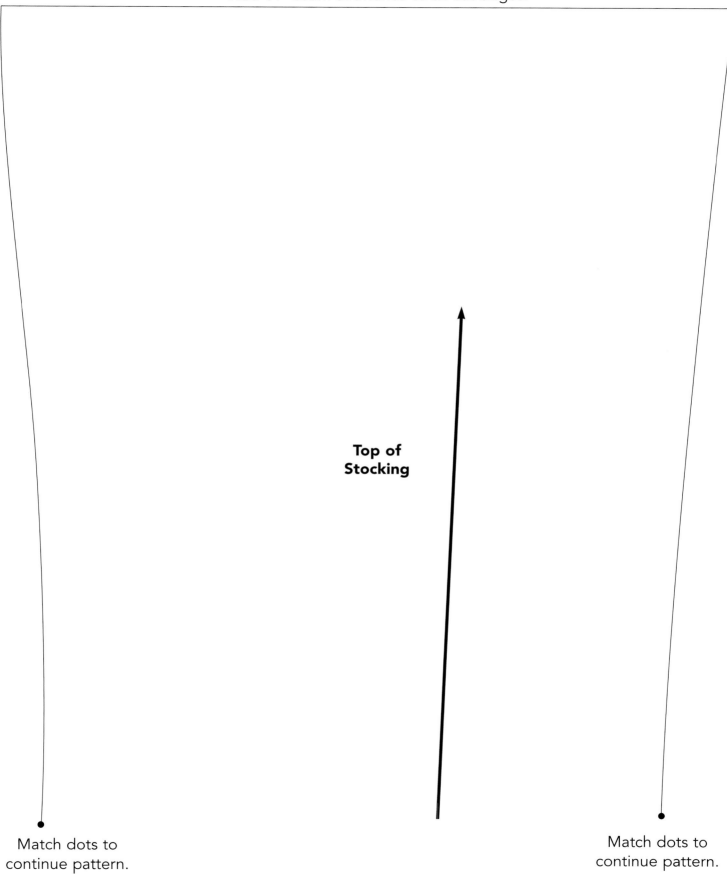

**Top of
Stocking**

Match dots to
continue pattern.

Match dots to
continue pattern.

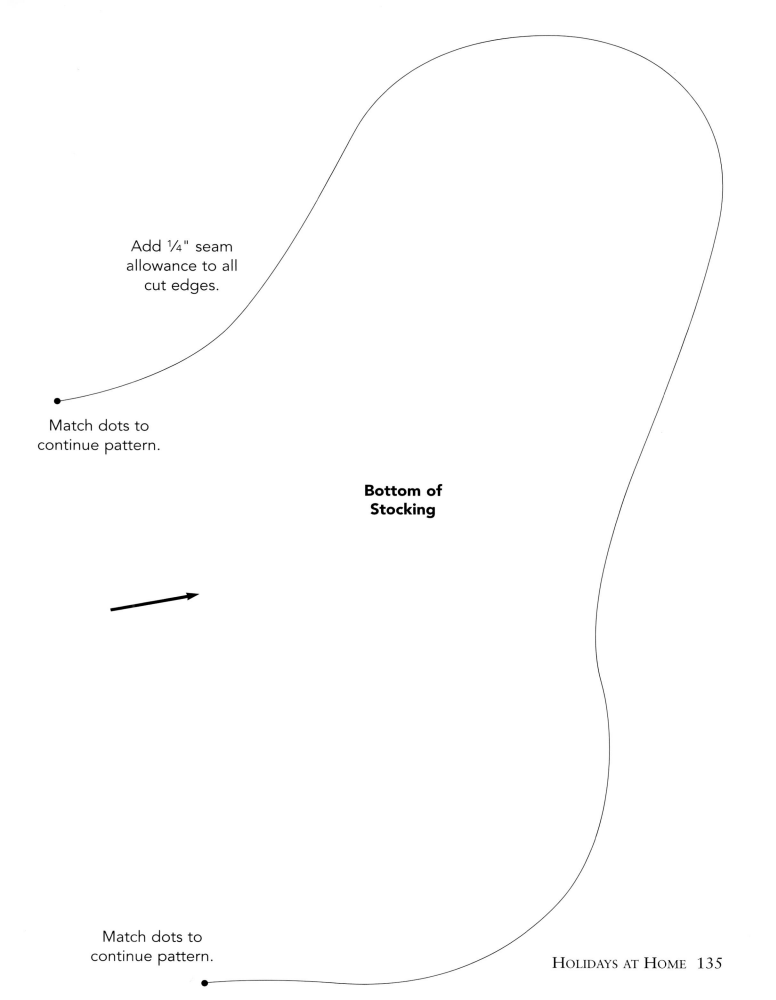

Add ¼" seam allowance to all cut edges.

Match dots to continue pattern.

Bottom of Stocking

Match dots to continue pattern.

Stitch & Stuff
Stars

A worn and damaged vintage quilt stages a shining comeback as patchwork stars. String a galaxy together for a wreath or a garland or sprinkle them around as package toppers.

Materials

For each star:

5½" square quilt remnant, with batting and
   backing removed

5½" square print or solid fabric for backing

Thread to match fabric

Hand-sewing needle

Stuffing

Dried lavender (optional)

For wreath:

20" grapevine wreath

Small safety pins (optional)

Ribbon scraps

For package topper:

Ribbon

Small safety pin

For garland:

Small safety pins (optional)

Instructions

Note: Seam allowances are ¼".

1. **For each star,** trace star pattern onto quilt remnant and fabric square. Cut out shapes along pattern lines. With right sides facing and raw edges aligned, stitch stars together, leaving opening for turning and stuffing. Clip curves; turn. Stuff firmly, adding lavender if desired. Slipstitch opening closed.

2. **For wreath,** make 12 stars. Connect stars, end to end, with safety pins or hand-stitch together. Tie stars to wreath with ribbon scraps.

3. **For package topper,** tie package with ribbon. Use small safety pin to attach star to ribbon.

4. **For garland,** make 12 stars. Connect stars, end to end, with safety pins or hand-stitch together. Tuck garland into tree branches as desired.

Star

Season's Greetings
Tree Skirt

This colorful tree skirt will become a treasure you look forward to unpacking every Christmas season.

Materials

Pencil
String
Thumbtack
45" square piece paper for making tree skirt pattern (Tape pieces together, if necessary, to obtain correct size.)
Fabrics: 2⅝ yards 45"-wide for tree skirt; ¼ yard each blue, green, and red
Disappearing-ink fabric marker
Straight pins
11 yards green braid
Thread to match tree skirt fabric and braid
1 yard paper-backed fusible web
Dimensional fabric paints: green, navy, silver

Instructions

Note: Seam allowances are ⅜".

1. To make paper pattern, tie pencil to end of string. Measure and mark 22½" from pencil and insert thumbtack into string at mark. Lay paper on flat surface. Insert thumbtack into center of paper. Pull string taut and draw 45"-diameter circle. Remove thumbtack, reinsert 2" from pencil, and then reinsert into center of paper. Pull string taut and draw 4"-diameter circle (Diagram 1 on page 140). Cut out both circles.

2. Cut tree-skirt fabric in half lengthwise. Lay pattern on right side of 1 tree-skirt fabric piece. Using disappearing-ink marker, mark outer and inner circles. Remove pattern; *do not* cut out yet. Repeat to mark remaining tree-skirt fabric piece. For tree-skirt top, on 1 marked tree-skirt piece, mark circle 3" in from outer edge; mark second circle 2½" in from previous circle (Diagram 2 on page 140).

3. Fold fabric for tree-skirt top in half and then in half again to divide skirt into quarters. Mark quarter sections with pins. Referring to Diagram 3 on page 140, at quarter marks, center and mark 2½" sections for each letter of word that will go in section. With disappearing-ink marker, write words on tree skirt in marked sections, using marked circles as guide for letter height. (Do not extend words into seam allowances.) Draw wavy lines to connect words. Between words "joy" and "cheer," draw straight line connecting edge of center circle with outer edge for tree skirt opening.

4. Tie knot in 1 end of green braid. Trim end to ½" and fringe. Beginning on 1 side of marked opening line, pin braid to tree-skirt top, following marked wavy lines and words. Machine-stitch braid in place. Satin-stitch dot at top of "j."

5. Trace 6 stars, 6 ornaments, and 6 packages (see pages 140 and 141) onto paper-backed fusible web. Roughly cut out shapes. On wrong side of fabrics, press star shapes onto blue, ornaments onto green, and packages onto red. Cut out shapes along pattern lines. Remove paper backing. Referring to photo, equally space shapes around tree skirt. (Bottoms of packages are 8" from outer marked edge of tree skirt, and bottoms of stars and ornaments are 8½" in from outer marked edge of tree skirt.) Fuse shapes in place, being careful not to iron over any fabric marking lines. (Heat from iron may set marks, making them difficult to remove.)

6. Staystitch ¼" in from marked outer and center circles and along both sides of opening line. Cut out tree skirt along marked lines. On undecorated tree-skirt fabric piece, draw straight line from edge of inner circle to outer circle. Cut out tree skirt; then cut along marked straight line. With right sides together, outer edges aligned, and edges of straight opening aligned, stitch ⅜" from all cut edges, leaving 8" unstitched along 1 edge of straight opening line for turning. Clip curved edges, trim corners, and turn right side out.

7. Remove fabric marking lines. Press tree skirt. Use green paint to outline packages, navy paint to outline stars, and silver paint to outline ornaments and to draw caps and hanging loops. Let dry.

8. For tree-skirt ties, cut 2 (12") pieces from remaining green braid. Tie knot in ends of each piece. Tack 1 braid piece to back of tree skirt at each end of inner circle.

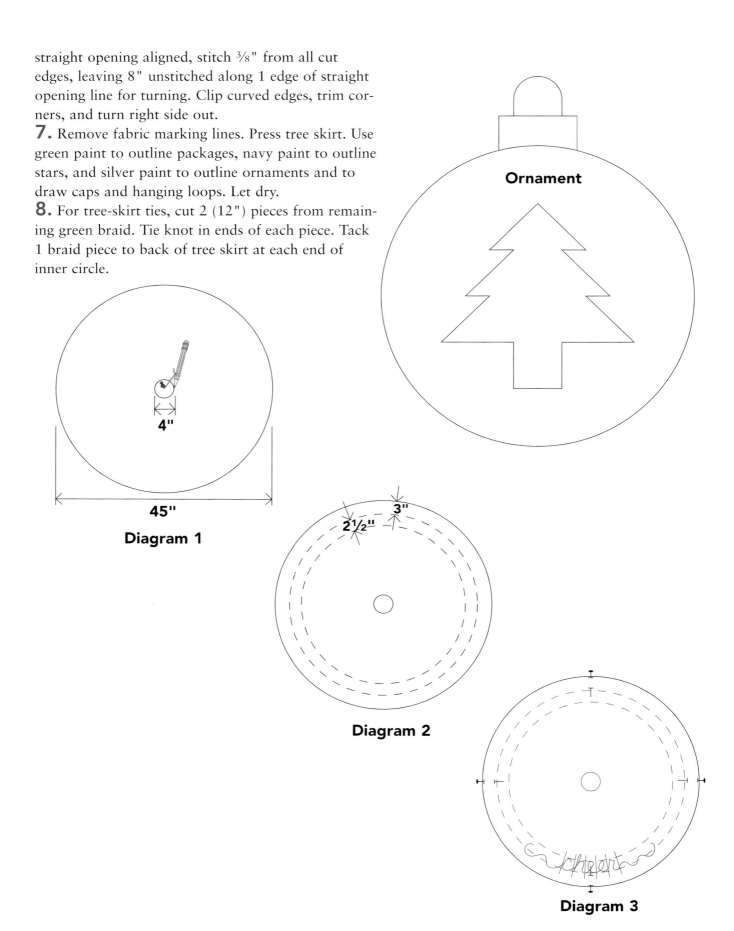

Ornament

4"

45"

Diagram 1

2½"   **3"**

Diagram 2

Diagram 3

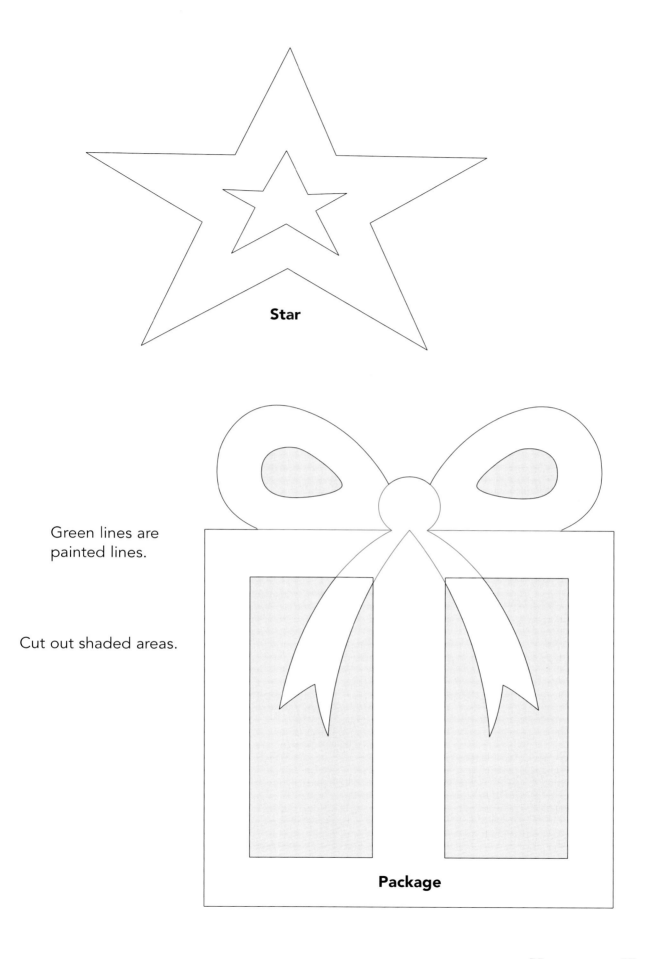

Star

Green lines are
painted lines.

Cut out shaded areas.

Package

Mitten
Guest Towel

Let your holiday decorations spill over into every room—even the bathroom. The motifs on this towel bring warmth to your home throughout the winter season.

Materials
Heavyweight paper-backed fusible web scraps
Plaid flannel scraps
Purchased towel
Red pearl cotton
Tapestry needle
2 (3") lengths ¼"-wide black velvet ribbon
Fabric glue
2 (½") blue buttons

Instructions
1. Press fusible web onto wrong side of flannel scraps. Trace 3 pairs of mittens onto paper side of flannel scraps. **For heart-embellished mittens,** trace 2 hearts onto paper side of coordinating flannel scrap. **For each,** cut out shapes along pattern lines. Remove paper backing. Referring to photo, position mittens on 1 short end of towel. Fuse mittens in place. Fuse hearts in place on top of 1 pair of mittens.

2. Referring to photo, use red pearl cotton and tapestry needle to backstitch mitten strings (see General Instructions on page 7).

3. Tie knot in center of each velvet ribbon length. Referring to photo, glue knots to cuffs of 1 pair of mittens. Trim ends of ribbon if necessary. Cut 2 (5") lengths of pearl cotton. Thread 1 end of 1

pearl cotton length through 1 buttonhole. Tie pearl cotton in knot at front of button. Repeat with remaining button. Trim ends of pearl cotton. Referring to photo, glue buttons to cuffs of remaining unembellished mittens. Let dry.

4. To launder, machine wash gentle cycle and dry on low temperature.

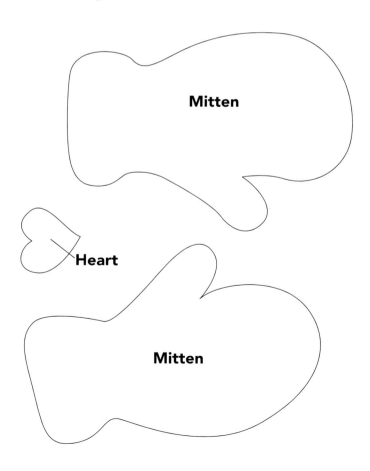

Mitten

Heart

Mitten

Acknowledgments

SPECIAL THANKS . . .

. . . to the following people for their valuable contributions toward project development:

Kim Eidson Crane: Tree-Trimmed Sweatshirt

Amanda Hagood: Stitch & Stuff Stars

Linda Hendrickson: Merry Pillow Wraps, Old-fashioned Batting Ornaments

Margot Hotchkiss: Herbal Bathtub Tea, Mother's Day Garden Tote, Ribbon Wreath

Alisa Jane Hyde: Candy Corn Table Accessories, Greeting Card Holder, Harvest Basket and Bread Cloth, Luck-of-the-Irish Dish Towel, Packaging Pouches, Pyramid Wrap, Turkey Pot Holder

Heidi Tyline King: All Boxed Up, Reverse Collage Holiday Plates, Sheer Happiness Cards

Duffy Morrison: Christmas Coasters, Jingle Jolly Stocking, Peppermint Stress-Relief Collar, Velvet Topiary

Dondra G. Parham: Dressy Bunnies, Festive Frames, Pillow for Pop, Pretty Package Place Mat

Catherine B. Pewitt: Easy Easter Totes, Fall Refrigerator Fun, Haunted Hangers, Tabletop Easter Pots, Valentine Photo Mats

Betsy Cooper Scott: Easter Banner, Happy Spider Halloween Shirt, Jack-o'-lantern Tote Bags, Poinsettia Pot Wraps, Spirited Mailbox Cover

Carol Tipton: Snowman Tree Topper, Sock It to the Seasons, Spring Chick Pillowcase

Sally Waldrop: Delightful Dish Towels

Patricia G. Weaver: Wonderful Wine Bags

Cynthia Moody Wheeler: Elegant Envelope Tablecloth, Falling Leaves Blanket, Independence Day Apron, Old Glory Place Mat, Patriotic Picnic Basket, Season's Greetings Tree Skirt

Peggy Ann Williams: Hanukkah Pillow, Heavenly Hearts, O Christmas Tree

Nancy Worrell: Autumn Leaf Table Runner, Christmas Carryall, Easter Baby Outfit, Mitten Guest Towel, New Year's Eve Confetti Tablecloth